Playing the University Game

ALSO AVAILABLE FROM BLOOMSBURY

Successful Dissertations, *edited by Caron Carter*
Writing a Watertight Thesis, *edited by Mike Bottery and Nigel Wright*
Taking Control of Writing Your Thesis, *Kay Guccione and Jerry Wellington*
Research Methods for Social Justice and Equity in Education, *Liz Atkins and Vicky Duckworth*
Pursuing Teaching Excellence in Higher Education, *Margaret Wood and Feng Su*
Social Theory and the Politics of Higher Education, *edited by Mark Murphy, Ciaran Burke, Cristina Costa and Rille Raaper*
Education, Music, and the Lives of Undergraduates, *Roger Mantie and Brent C. Talbot*
Non-University Higher Education, Holly Henderson
Transforming University Education, *Paul Ashwin*
Reflective Teaching in Higher Education, *Paul Ashwin with David Boud, Susanna Calkins, Kelly Coate, Fiona Hallett, Gregory Light, Kathy Luckett, Jan McArthur, Iain McLaren, Monica McLean, Velda McCune, Katarina Mårtensson and Michelle Tooher*
Fostering Self-Efficacy in Higher Education Students, *Laura Ritchie*
Understanding Experiences of First Generation University Students, *edited by Amani Bell and Lorri J. Santamaría*
The Good University, *Raewyn Connell*
Negotiating Learning and Identity in Higher Education, *edited by Bongi Bangeni and Rochelle Kapp*
Why Universities Should Seek Happiness and Contentment, *Paul Gibbs*

Playing the University Game

The Art of University-Based Self-Education

HELEN E. LEES

BLOOMSBURY ACADEMIC
LONDON • NEW YORK • OXFORD • NEW DELHI • SYDNEY

BLOOMSBURY ACADEMIC
Bloomsbury Publishing Plc
50 Bedford Square, London, WC1B 3DP, UK
1385 Broadway, New York, NY 10018, USA
29 Earlsfort Terrace, Dublin 2, Ireland

BLOOMSBURY, BLOOMSBURY ACADEMIC and the Diana logo are trademarks of
Bloomsbury Publishing Plc

First published in Great Britain 2022

For legal purposes the Acknowledgements on p. viii constitute an extension of this
copyright page.

Cover design: Charlotte James
Cover image © Mark Weiss/ Getty Images

A catalogue record for this book is available from the British Library.

A catalog record for this book is available from the Library of Congress.

ISBN: HB: 978-1-3501-8848-8
PB: 978-1-3501-8847-1
ePDF: 978-1-3501-8845-7
eBook: 978-1-3501-8846-4

Typeset by Deanta Global Publishing Services, Chennai, India

To find out more about our authors and books visit www.bloomsbury.com and sign up
for our newsletters.

WARNING ABOUT UNIVERSITIES

Universities are tricky and complicated. They require you to step out of your comfort zone, to be challenged, to take risks of thought. To travel and explore, to be humble, a beginner, a student. To defer. All within an apparent context of prestige, excellence, achievement and of 'their' success. Universities require you to think and think again and no longer know what you thought you knew. To be, no longer, who you were. To become. Like them. That is part of the joy of a university experience. It is a ride. It is an acquisition. But it can be explosive. It can hurt to change. It can hurt to come to know. To lose yourself to seemingly gain yourself. Exchange yourself. This book has your safety in mind because no one should get lost in a university nor in the idea of what a university could be. You are precious just the way you are. Acquire. Don't expire.

Contents

Acknowledgements

I would like to thank the intelligent, brave, caring academics who contributed their conversations to this book; all the interesting and important students I have spoken with over the years of my engagement in higher education; the scholars who have written inspiring, great work about the university as contestable and in difficulties. I warmly thank Alison Baker and her colleagues at Bloomsbury, including reviewers, for their various forms of support and development of this project. In particular, Karen Butler, who helped me understand the requirement that we all have to take responsibility for ourselves, is someone to whom I owe deep gratitude.

Introducing the Game We Play

This book is about how to play the university game. Inevitably, how to win. Not play and win against the odds nor win against others through competition. This is about how to play and then win something precious and meaningful for yourself, as easily as possible and with joy, within a community that matters to you and to others. Whatever to win might be, or mean to you personally, inter-relationally, it is a good thing because it is positive. It's also a good thing because one way or another university involvement costs people a lot. Either money, usually in large amounts, or substantial life sacrifices – likely both – are almost always involved in being associated with a university. So winning is a good outcome for these various forms of investment and losing anything except ignorance, well, it's not what we want.

Universities can present to students a significant, sometimes bamboozling, challenge that can become an unenjoyable difficulty, if you are not prepared. This book seeks to avoid university-based negativity hurting you. A protective self-education is at hand here, not only dealing with the complexity of the university and its many levels and layers but also acknowledging that you yourself are complex and consist of many interlocking parts. Possibly the most challenging aspect for you of the university game is that a lack of compassionate humanity (which is very much needed for beginner players in any game) is not just *a part* of university experience, it is a defining characteristic of all layers and levels. It is an inhumanity without personal attention or care that is so embedded it serves – especially in recent times – as a function of how universities work. Who are you in all of this? The university will not provide the answer. Finding that answer and doing so meaningfully and with joy is something you have to do for yourself, through self-education. Enter not therein unprepared because university institutions aren't, it feels, *that* bothered about their inhumanity as a function. Even when various reports, publications and internal institutional complaints, formal and informal, around the world showcase these challenges, universities seemingly carry on largely regardless, their eye to the bottom line. Perhaps 'challenges' is the wrong word and 'dysfunctions' might be a better choice. I think they don't focus on it because the difficulties I'm talking about affect the heart, the personal level of university experience and your Self, none of which are, it seems, considered 'university business' in any profound way. But these personal layers of what you encounter when you attend a university ought to be attended to, because going to university is your unique experience and *very* personally affecting. That ought to be a good affect.

In this book we *are* bothered about that affect, because we care about ourselves. We are going to work it, work the university game, as it is offered. We are quite literally going to play them at their own game and win but on terms of self-care and compassion. You will win because you matter and you will win in the face of the 'challenges', rather than by attempting to get universities to change themselves. This book is about dealing with the 'dark academia' (Fleming 2021) reality just hinted at earlier through focusing on what is good and right and identifying the strategic play. Because it is a game it is also good fun. Puzzles are enjoyable.

To see the game as a puzzle and one that can be solved or won or, at the very least, thoroughly enjoyed is, frankly, a therapeutic element in the face of the potentially impersonal journey to obtaining university 'success'. We do that via the idea of you being in charge of your own education and that protecting you. Some prospective or current students may be reading this and not really understand what I mean by needing a protective education about universities, but they might. Academic staff may be well aware of my meaning. All told, the conversations in this book are designed to provide – for the initiate and the weary – a start, or boost, to understanding and awareness and to taking protective care of oneself. And the book is also *designed* to do this by avoiding being a teacher but rather acting as a facilitator of knowledge of some 'rules' – it's very hard to play a game with any gusto if you have no 'instruction booklet' to facilitate your moves. You also can gain an understanding here in how to self-educate further, *beyond* this book, about your university investments. You gain value through reading this book for what it means to learn to continually learn, in order to navigate those spaces and their demands. This is so you can enjoy yourself by being in control of what you know. That self-educating attitude will serve you well beyond your university time. The skills acquired through *this* game can helpfully equip you in the future or help you help yourself and others, elsewhere and in different circumstances.

In the following chapters, some written and unwritten rules of the game are offered, either via conversations held between myself and some academic colleagues or through a collection of notes presented. So many things to think about. Not only is there a system of admissions, merit, privilege, equalizing, access and many other factors of being at a university in the first place, but inside the university space there are politics, positions and power. These are socio-material considerations: what we need to navigate as facts of university life and university function-dysfunction, so to speak. They are aspects to negotiate. Often they are issues to overcome or deal with: even, at times, battle out of necessity, in order to ensure you get the care you deserve and need. While the 'rules' simplify these, they are focused mostly at another level: that of the personal level within this complexity. Other rules not here exist but those presented are a kick-starter kit to finding your way in, of and out of the idea of rules, so that a game, playing it, being played, all become easier. The personal is political, but it is also what you live with, colouring every moment. Moments you would prefer were nice to experience. So, the general idea of listening to 'rules' is there in order to help you make your personal life lived in the university environment calm and collected. Despite how universities actually operate to avoid the personal as much as possible – their business, after all, being the sciences of knowledge, not you – I see you and your personal as a science worth valuing. I see your personal as a web of significance and worth, intrinsic to any and all forms of knowledge. Universities would rather sidestep this unique web of yours and concentrate on money, knowledge and power as a matrix. The rules I offer are to ensure that your personal experience matters, given the game and the environment we are dealing with. They position you actively and positively at the heart of the university matrix, not as a passive acolyte. This is not a stance of individualism I am taking here where an individual gets to be selfishly ahead or egotistically beefed up. The perspective we are working with, as we self-educate in and through this book about university experience, is of community. There is no good community to be within, express ourselves within, care for ourselves and others within, if people are anxious, unfulfilled, unhappy and confused. Winning at university is a profound struggle for many students. I dislike this dynamic. It isn't fair and it isn't right. I have created this book to intervene in that situation by leveraging the personal Self as a form of power students can gain for traction in the university.

The Game

There are many aspects of the game, many stages and many moves. Most involve money somewhere because whether studying, teaching or researching, somebody's money is required to fund these. But the scholarship involved in study or teaching and research activity is another side; it is its own world and one where education as activity should rule, not money. Reputation and social position, yours and the university's, is a powerful player in this game. Success, whatever that means, in all its actual relativity, is another. Knowledge – very contestable knowledge, scientism, white, male, Western scientism – is another. All of it is mentioned, paid its due necessary attention and then it is ignored. We will be busy with better things.

Because universities are institutions, they aren't someone you can approach, regard, seek to understand and then reason with or intuitively get a feel for the possibilities 'between you'. As buildings, systems, styles, courses, bills to pay, agendas, politics, policies, places, seminars, meetings to attend and hoops to jump through, universities are not there to care for you. So we need to notice, note, not ignore all of the politics large and small and deliberately focus on our own well-being by then ignoring this as just so much fluff.

Although universities might actually wish to care about you, they cannot alas because they are systems. They are also very managerial, meaning into various statistical targets (Collini 2017). To not matter yourself much and yet think the university matters a lot is a tough dynamic: a painful one to encounter and to bear. Don't bear such a dynamic. Drop it.

Universities are useful. That's it. This book largely assumes they *can* be useful in some way or ought to be, if they are fulfilling their role as a university and if you work out an equalized dynamic to your satisfaction. *Make* them useful to you. Giving of yourself to a university at the personal level as a kind of fantasy relationship (a common situation because universities are sexy) is not wise. What do you gain from that? In Chapter 2, I talk about university fantasy as a bad idea and not fantasizing about the great and good university as a good idea. A university is not a person and it won't look you in the eye when you meet. It may do worse. The conversation transcripts in this book give a taste of that disregard.

This book is to help you equalize the dynamic between yourself and the university. It is just a book and it isn't the only answer and it isn't all the answers. It does not want to be. Why not the grand saviour for distress? Because the right and best answers come from you and *your* working out of them. You are unique, as will be your answers and your ways to handle things. One of the best things about being in a university is the time it gives you to work things out for yourself. Unfettered time for you, we could say, so it is important you benefit as much as time allows. That kind of freedom from other obligations is rare in a lifetime.

So this book is about how to succeed, on your terms. For your needs and your ends. Getting through and getting through well, each day, possibly every day. Making the most of university. This 'making the most' has, I believe, a special formula: writing. Not just any writing but your writing, contextualized in 'their' knowledge (the canon, the archive, the state of the art, the cutting edge, the desired-to-be-known unknowns) such that your writing becomes their knowledge and thus your knowledge. That is a process the conversations which follow discuss. Do they give you detailed, irrefutable instructions, step by step? No. Why not? Because that process is not written in stone and nor should it be. It is your process.

If the answer to playing this university game well is, broadly speaking, 'take care of yourself', what does that have to do with being in a university beyond the standard advice to eat healthily and get some decent sleep? I don't mean those things, although I include them as vital for other forms of self-care to work. I'm talking about avoiding the university hurting your feelings through its systematized institutional disregard because you are taking care of your heart. Taking care of your heart is to take care of your mind. If you have yourself at the centre of care and activity you will be self-collected and well grounded. All of this is about education. Then you will be able to read well and with best speed, write coherently and make decent arguments that you enjoy making. That's what gets you through university as a formal winner: care about self to care about writing. Universities are machineries for writing and if you enter in you had better appreciate that fact.

But when you enter in the sometimes brutal environment of the university, where fragility, error and ignorance are to lose and be a loser, you might be dismayed to find your inevitable neophyte weakness is seen as bad. But it isn't bad at all. It's human, humane, normal and a fundamental characteristic of what it means to learn, to grow and to come to know. It is also inevitable because, as Schwartz (2021) says, we are all partly struggling, most of the time. If I'm not mistaken, the purpose of higher education is to expand people and knowledge from a position of relative ignorance? Oh good. So we're on track and in the right place.

Believe that to be a student is beautiful. Your weakness in a university space is beautiful. It is, coupled with a desire to understand the world better, your special power. It is what makes you a good and interesting student. Otherwise known as necessary scholarly humility. Please remember that when you feel little in a seminar or lecture room.

Resistance

I know universities are not *good* enough and so do many others. There is fear and trembling involved in the playing, woven into the fabric of the academy (Hall and Bowles 2016; Hall 2021). I envision a better university where people matter more than prestige, where negative games of drama triangles (Karpman 2007, 2014) are not evident around every corner, and where the heart, emotions included, has as much status as the mind. This book is my way to get us playing the game in and of university life differently, like we personally, truly and beautifully matter, just the weak, developing, imperfect, wonderful, talented, intellectually curious and alive way we are. Alas to speak thus is to call for a counter-cultural revolutionary call to arms. Which is astonishing. It betrays the state of universities that asking for an atmosphere that is humane goes against the current tide of how universities treat people inhumanely (Hall and Bowles 2016; Smyth 2018; Brennan and Magness 2019;

Mayo 2019; Meyerhoff 2019; McCallam 2020; Fleming 2021; Hall 2021). But that is what we are asking for and indeed, through playing differently, we can create another university. We can get through well.

In this book you will find stories, advice, perspectives – from expert academic minds who each have reflected deeply and personally on the university, through years of experience – allowing you to think yourself to the centre of care and self-led education in university spaces and to effectively resist. These narratives, in the form of conversations to which you are very warmly invited, as if to a small and extremely friendly seminar space, armour you, they prepare you, they empower you. They support students, amid all the fanfare about universities as elite, awesome places of aspiration, to ground themselves in forms of truth telling. Given staff at universities are suffering significant negative effects of stress in their workplaces for various reasons (Morrish 2019) the narratives here can also serve them, as they are designed to serve students who are stressed out and wondering. Truth telling is, as Michel Foucault said, a 'regime' (Foucault 1977) involving 'techniques of power' (Foucault 1980: 125) and those who tell hold the power. Let's be true.

So our game – to self-educate to self-care and self-care to self-educate through using the university for which you pay dearly – is in a moral, social and political context which, if we were to be a little on the pessimistic side, we could call 'difficult'. Universities assume 'epistemic and moral authority' within a world system in crisis but are entirely culpable in being part of 'the underlying violence and unsustainability of that system' (Stein 2020). They have a vested interest in maintaining the status quo. Note to yourself: this is not an easy game.

My focus then is to enable the emotional, psychological and spiritual price of attending university to be both comfortably payable and fairly achieved. Lew, Huen et al. (2019: 2) speak of a 'tense campus climate' as a feature of a university environment and mention suicides. Hall calls the university an 'anxiety machine' (Hall 2014). These scholars link this tense machinery to some students and staff falling *inevitably* into grave mental health difficulties. It's not healthy nor helpful to hang around tension. Because the university represents success and *being* success in a wider system it really matters how you experience it because you do not want tense environments impacting enjoyment of your university time and your life chances. In connecting yourself then to a university by attending for a course of study the stakes are high. If you fall short or fail in the university you fall short on a wider, lifelong, social and potentially economic scale. I am a teacher and an academic educationist with a specialism in what alternatives to a violent[1] education *system* there might be. This makes me interested to know how education as a system, which is part of wider societal systems, can *avoid* being poisonous in climate and experience, thereby harming people. It too often is poison

(Pilkington and Piersel 1991; Carlen et al. 1992; Yoneyama 1999; Yoneyama and Naito 2003; Harber 2004; Peim and Flint 2009; Flint and Peim 2012; Peim 2012; Lees 2014). It too often harms people, too much and too deeply. Although there is something to be said for imperfection, difficulty, disappointment and ambiguity in education (Tsabar 2014, 2021), we are playing the university game to ensure that accidental, impersonal tension from outside ourselves is not inner, personalized damage.

Education positions people in a binary – good, bad, strong, weak, win, lose, succeed, fail, stupid, intelligent, fit, unfit, appropriate, inappropriate (Lees 2012). People suffer from *not* being either a binary '1 or 0'. Of course they are not 0 or 1 because they are people. People are not code in a computer programme. It hurts people's feelings, apart from anything else, to be reduced like this. Universities as a part of a 'binarized' (dichotomous) education system are involved in this hurt alas. To counteract this positioning of people one way or the other in a competitive frame it is ironic that we need to play to win, is it not? But our game here is designed in a special way to sidestep binaries and their positioning: playing the way this book advocates is through writing, as previously mentioned, but it also uses the power of education and educating oneself to help you rise above the nonsense of being labelled.

Resistance against education in action as harm is required, individually, collectively. If this book aims to interact with the status quo it is only – but this is never 'only' in a university context – by being honest and straightforward. There is resistance in fearless speech (Foucault 2001). Through reading this book you encounter respect for student and staff power, voice and choice, as the other way to know a university. Listen first to the voices in this book and then reflect for yourself on it all. You may or may not agree, and collegiate dissent is part of universities when they are going right. If powerful forces that dehumanize, label, sift and sort individuals are to be resisted because they don't care about your brilliance (you are brilliant), then a *self-determined* identity as a student of the university must be forged and enjoyed. This is, as always, about power, but here the power is generated from within, not accumulated from without. Your inner self is powerfully articulate and deeply enabled to protect you. It is a powerful player in the university game. It does not have its power from the university matrix but is the natural power of people born as full of inherent energy, excellence and potential.

Writing Matters Most as Your Sports Equipment[2]

The university needs writing. It functions through mechanisms of showing writing (or other disciplinary relevant assessment methods for which writing stands as a symbol). This means that you need to read, reflect, write, submit and wait for feedback, including your assessment mark. It's all about performance. This performance is relative: you are either the best or the worst or relative to either extreme. It isn't a university system that wants to enjoy your writing without this framework around it. The university needs that framework to make sense of and to judge your writing so it can measure it along the spectrum of success and failure. Hard-nosed it is, but hopefully fair (see rule 2, in Chapter 2). By focusing on writing as the key, overall and strategically encompassing 'rule of the game', I suggest you can turn the university system to your advantage.

The trick is to find a way to enjoy the writing task and create of it a vehicle for self-expression. In a university, there are standards of presentation, some standards of academic manner such as no plagiarism, an emphasis on original thought, using the right style of citation, scholarship, reading, researching, discussion and so forth. These manners can all be taught and universities are duty-bound to provide support with these mechanistic aspects that, if got wrong, can drag the important creative parts down, affecting marks or outcomes holding value. But ultimately writing is also without rules and without prior known destination: it is a mystery and an adventure. Through writing, by reflecting and thinking of and within positions of thought that matter, a person can fly and find intellectual ecstasy. No joke. Try it out. Your voice is interesting.

Universities are uniquely positioned to provide access to a context of other people, within which you can try out that voice that is uniquely yours. An audience, your performance. This is helpful and the special talent of a university: to provide context for the written, thoughtful voice of anyone. This book allows you to set yourself and your writing in a context of understanding of the game that writing is, within the game that a university is, which itself sits within a game of social success and, of course, all of this sits within the greatest game of all: attending to self with kindness and curiosity about what you want to say.

A Complex Journey to Enjoyment

In speaking with seven experts of students' experience (all connected to students as university academic teachers and guides) about the project of this book as a way for you to avoid suffering negative drama, I came to understand the journey to enjoyment in universities is complex. It is not just mechanistically tied to writing great essays and thus overcoming difficulties, as I had, at first, thought. That is why this book is the Russian Doll of university experience somewhat unpacked, rather than an instrumental guide to writing. The game is not just about writing well and ignoring the rest. Things worth having, herein seen as satisfaction at profound personal growth, rather than a certificate, although that can matter too, are complicated to get. There is some comment about the university as toxic, negative, failing and a failure in the conversations. But there is also good news. After reading this book my hope is you will feel *empowered* to write. Thereby empowered to play and win the game. Writing requires work and application for sure, but if some of the emotional confusion of being a person who writes in a university has been cleared away, you stand a chance of succeeding to the best of your ability.

Very few students seem to have an education in the university game and I was surprised to discover how very little most students knew when I asked them about this. In the context of one of my university jobs lecturing about writing academically, I found myself talking with undergraduate and postgraduate students about the inside of academia and academic pursuits as a part of a university system of learning, writing, marking, assessments, grading. Students were fascinated to learn about this insider knowledge. Some students had no idea academics cared about them enough to share such information and were visibly surprised that I would speak frankly. When I opened up the Pandora's box of the mechanistic, emotional and political inside of the university, it seemed to be empowering those students. This knowledge seemed to set the writing they were having to do – some happily and enthusiastically and some with pain, loathing, fear – in a broader context of interest. The university is interesting after all, in and of itself, if you pay attention. It is also, whether student or staff, your vital and attentive interlocutor. It is, in its better guise and with the true, dedicated and valued academics of the university in mind, the audience for your writing performance and the voice within.

The Conversations

The colleagues of the university with whom I have significantly engaged in this book, in order to bring to you an insider perspective of the many layers of the inside of universities, are seven people. It is not a survey of thousands. So the conversations must be appreciated as subjective and personal viewpoints. Yet these academics speak so openly and informedly – with their many years of hard-won experience – about what universities are. Frankly, their words pertain to situations found across the globe. They represent a distinctive, honest and reliable voice. I hope this book shows you *how much* some academics care about you, with people speaking who have focused attentively in what they say on enriching your experience and enabling your personal triumph. Every conversation is different; each is very stimulating. The transcripts together offer a 'hidden transcript'; a 'critique of power spoken behind the back of the dominant' force that is the university (Scott 1990: xii); or rather here, to its face. This book aims to be one of 'those rare moments of political electricity when, often for the first time in memory, the hidden transcript is spoken directly and publicly in the teeth of power' (Scott 1990: xiii). All we do here is talk honestly in front of you, the student. No drama.

A Note about the Conversation Contributors

All the contributors are established scholars, with well over a 100 years of experience of university life and university-student interactions to draw on. They do not all speak English as a first language but all worked at the time of the conversations in English-medium institutions. Three live and work in North America and four in the UK. Obviously, these factors affect what they know and what they say. Unless otherwise stated, they speak under a pseudonym, a measure which I, as author of this book, deemed appropriate as an ethical protocol. I have *not* given rank and position details to do with their job. Each voice speaks from personal experience linked to what might well be *your* experience. Every person speaking is someone who, in some ways, is like you. Without meeting you, they clearly, either by virtue of their vocation as a university teacher or collegially, emotionally and in spirit, stand in solidarity with you.

The conversations were transcribed as a whole and then lightly edited but not changed or reduced, unless by the contributor, who maintained control of the text throughout the writing up process. Transcriptions were sent to each contributor for review, possible edits and final approval before they were published. Ethical protocols concerning anonymized treatment of data, right to withdraw and other aspects of research done ethically were followed and communicated.

Coda

None of this 'safeguarding' inherent in learning to play to win would either matter or be necessary if universities were businesses with a bottom line, whose bottom line we were forced to accept as the key priority. While universities (and governments) might behave thus – as if education were a commodity – I and many others in the educational game refute that university education is a commodity. We do not accept their conditions. University education is an exchange. Not only that but it is definitively and irrefutably a personal and interpersonal exchange of great spiritual, moral and social value *involving equality between students and staff*. It is not a business transaction of any kind, despite money changing hands. In an atmosphere of universities as knowledge-education businesses, safeguarding is required. We need to *protect* both self and education from the abuse of self and education that universities-as-businesses perpetrate.

For Students

What You Need to Know

Know yourself: past experiences and their impact on the present
Know yourself: preferred study methods
Give yourself time for tasks and then some spare
Read around to explore a variety of topics and interests
Take notes as you read and listen and keep your notes organized
Prepare for encounters/meetings with academics: attend these having
shared, in advance, something written
Do a subject you find, in general, personally interesting
Do not engage with drama – seek solutions to difficulties
Be honest about vulnerability and state your needs to those who can help
Look after yourself – health, eating, sleeping, exercise
Do not believe the university
Do not fantasize about the university
See the university not as an institution, but as individual people
Use the university
Notice the facilities of the university and engage with them if you wish
Visit the library/libraries often and respect them
Use silence respectfully for yourself and others
Treat intoxication with caution
Be careful with money
Enjoy your mood, whatsoever it might be
Breathe, look up!
Ground yourself literally by touching the earth with your body
To self-educate at university level do this:

Think for and with yourself.
Know for yourself.
Care for yourself.
Read for and with yourself.
Discuss, share, explore.
Write for and with yourself.
Enjoy.

What You Need to Have

A timetable to organize attendance at lectures, seminars, workshops
A timetable to self-organize study and academic skills development
Information on submission deadlines, exam dates, term dates
Stationary infrastructure to organize your work and records
A reasonably fast computer with as decent an internet access as possible
An institutional library entrance card
Reference management software (e.g. Endnote, Refworks, Mendeley –
check first what is used at your university as that version is the one they will
support and train you with. They all do the same basic job. Some are free
and some for a payment)
A copy of the marking criteria guidelines of your university for examiners of
submitted summative work in your subject – having this will enable you to
know what is required to get the mark you want
Opinions that you form and express
Feedback (as a tool)
A sense of humour
Patience
Self-esteem
Self-forgiveness
Self-belief
A mode of transporting yourself distances with a vehicle
A watch or other time-keeping device
Suitable clothes and food to maintain health
Some friends to talk with

1

Navigating the University

*T*his conversation happened between myself and Eli Meyerhoff after the profound affect reading his book (mentioned in the following paragraphs) had on my thinking about students playing the university game. His point of view transformed my approach to the university by 360 degrees and has affected this book significantly. I was shocked by the change and the revelation Eli's thinking offers because what he says is obviously true and yet this is, somehow, not available information for students. It is very appropriate that the conversation with him begins the journey, inherent in the discussions between myself and others in this book, of raising student awareness of the hidden university. In this conversation universities are discussed as arrogant social devices. They are seen as dividing people, betraying people, using social pressures, all at a student's personal and emotional expense. You are challenged to fully consider your motivations for attending university. The personal price you can pay for not having the knowledge this conversation points towards is seen as too high. We talk about how there is a way to enjoy yourself at university in a meaningful, positive way and avoid the university cruelly using you. In large part that protective positivity – full of self-care through taking in new ideas – starts by reading this and the other conversations.

Helen: Eli, what do students need to enjoy themselves at university?

Eli: Great question. That's a question I wish I had thought about before I'd gone to university. Students should think about why they want to go to university. Think about what's motivating them, what's compelling them. They can ask themselves if their motivations are ones that they've chosen and justified for themselves or if they're being driven by forces they don't understand.

Just thinking back on my own experiences in educational institutions, I had a confusing mess of different motivations to go to university. It took me many years of fumbling around, experimenting, feeling frustrated and going through a lot of personal crises – trying out different pathways in the university, critically reflecting on these crises – before I really found some bearings for navigating universities in more enjoyable and meaningful ways. Those experiences motivated me to write my book *Beyond Education* (Meyerhoff 2019). In that book I came up with some new ways of understanding universities that could provide guidance for students thinking about how to navigate them.

If we see universities as concentrated collections of resources and means for studying (classrooms, computers, books, teachers, other student collaborators), then we can think about different *modes* of studying with those resources, different modes of engaging with them. I make a distinction between different modes of studying. The dominant mode of studying has been what we call 'education', which has several key elements. The first is a vertical imaginary: we imagine ourselves as individuals rising up the levels of education, from kindergarten through twelfth grade and up into higher education levels. A second element is the dichotomous or binary figures of education: some figures are seen as valuable, other figures are seen as wasteful or waste products. A key example is the figure of the graduate, in opposition to the figure of the dropout. The dropout takes on a negative image compared to the vertical imaginary, as dropping out of that rising pathway. A third element of education is that students are separated from the means for studying. Their access to those means tends to be mediated by teachers and administrators. A fourth element is that individuals are shaped with a kind of emotional economy of shame, pride and anxiety that has been institutionalized with practices of grading, grades and exams. A fifth key element of education is that it prepares students to be participants in the dominant order: to go along with and participate in the dominant modes of governing and ordering of the world.

In my book, I give histories of how these elements came to be. How they can be collected together in institutions of education and seen as necessary, as the best and most important mode of studying, to the exclusion of alternatives. For students, to see how these elements of education have histories behind them, how they've been constructed, how they've come to be seen as natural and thinking about their history and thinking about possible alternatives, it can help students de-naturalize them. Unsettle, disrupt their sense of necessity, inevitability. To open up perspectives on alternatives. That kind of perspective, I think, can help students take a more critical or nuanced or self-made, self-motivated kind of approach to engaging with universities. They can ask themselves: What are the resources available for studying at a university? What are my motivations for engaging with those resources? They can ask about being pushed or motivated by desires: What have I been habituated to take on through my earlier experiences of education institutions? Desires like wanting to climb up this educational ladder towards a lucrative job in the world of work beyond school, beyond university, a kind of fighting to survive, motivated by anxieties and fears. Is it for them: Do I want to avoid the shame from being seen as a failure or dropout? Is it: A desire to gain esteem and pride in the eyes of my fellow classmates and teachers, my parents? I think in posing to themselves such questions students can critically reflect on whether those are the habits, desires that they want to be motivated by. Or do they want to choose different motivations, different desires for engaging with the means of studying in universities? I think that is one way students can approach a path to enjoyment on their own terms.

Helen: Can I ask you a question about the timings of everything? You suggested at the start of what you just said that you came to a new way of engaging with the idea of the university, of enjoying it, through the writing of your book *Beyond Education* (Meyerhoff 2019). But I know that you're forty something and you published the book two years ago? I guess the book, maybe, took four years to write?

Eli: I started working on it in my dissertation in 2007. I finished my dissertation in 2013, so that was six years of working with my dissertation. And then it took me five more years of writing a book.

Helen: So, it was a long process. Before that process began – because that process sounds like the solution to a set of anomalies and crisis points, or you could almost call it a therapeutic response, perhaps? – you were possibly like me. Maybe that's why we both have a similar interest in the areas that we've come to. You were, and this is a question: You were in existential trouble? You were in trouble vis-à-vis the forces that you speak of, of the world and how they create the desires that are perhaps not necessarily our own, for who we want to be and how we want to engage with the world? Could you tell students reading this book a bit about the trouble you were in?

Eli: Yeah. I felt like I was constantly trying to grapple with this kind of feeling of being stuck. I was stuck at a kind of impasse, working through some kind of trouble from feeling like the dominant world – in which I needed to survive – was messed up in a lot of ways: that it was causing harm, violence, pain to so many people, pain to myself and my friends. I felt like I wanted to do something. Something that could change that world, yet I felt I needed to get some kind of position to survive within that world at the same time. I guess the university – going to a higher level within the university – felt like a way to temporarily escape from having to make a decision about that. During my undergraduate years I started out as a chemical engineer. Then I escaped into philosophy, added a philosophy major. I worked as an engineer for a year after college, to make some money to pay off debts. Then I escaped that career path into graduate school, in philosophy. This gave a kind of space to try to grapple with that trouble as an impasse. To study it. Or to study the world more to try to figure out what to do about this kind of tense position of being critical of the world and trying to survive within it at the same time. I found that philosophy was too abstract, so I got into political theory. Political science, in fact, which was more practically focused in its use of theory, compared to the philosophy discipline. At the University of Minnesota, students and workers were organizing to improve their working, living and studying conditions. There was a clerical workers union that went on strike in 2007. I, as a graduate student, joined with some other students in supporting that strike. Some students organized a hunger strike in support of the workers' strike. Through that experience I saw the university itself as part of the broader world. I couldn't see it as a place to escape to anymore, because the violence of the broader world was part of the university itself. Questions about how to change the world could be applied to the university. That motivated me to focus my dissertation research on theorizing the political struggles at and around the university itself.

Helen: In that context of discovering that the university is part of – well, for the sake of this conversation, I'll call it – 'the drama of existence' in this world – it's not necessarily that the drama of existence would be the way it is in another world. It might be different. It might be better. It might be worse. But the specific drama of existence of this world that we have right now in 2020 or 2030 or whenever the moment is – this is what we deal with. This book talks about the university as being dramatic. I had this thesis that being at a university, students are encountering stress and personal drama, because *existence* is dramatic. But actually what I've discovered in the research for and writing of this book is that the university is itself a highly dramatic place. For various reasons to do with status, reputation, high stakes or so-called high stakes. Its position at the pinnacle, or the top of the Tree of Knowledge, as it pertains to the existence that we're, in fact, both talking about. The way that the game is played in a university – it all makes the university highly dramatic. But in a drama triangle, negative sense. Not a fruitful drama, as such. There isn't a drive in universities to defuse drama. Are they even riding it, for fun? So when an ordinary person – I mean otherwise undisturbed – I mean, they might be disturbed in one or two other areas, which is kind of normal, part of being a human being, being flawed, being in a flawed existence and so on – but then, when they enter into the university, those disturbances that they already inevitably had get added to, by the dramatic disturbing environment that we could say the university is as a personal experience. Thereby the university as dramatic makes the normal, existential personal drama of an ordinary person much more acute, much more pronounced. So it's not that students in the university are stressed, or they've got mental health issues that are *unresolvably* heavy. I'm saying this in the context of reports that student stress and mental health is bad and getting worse (see, e.g. Mistler et al. 2012; Coughlan 2015; September 30, LeViness et al. 2019; Morrish 2019). It's possibly that the university, the careless and care-less university, *makes* people more ill than they otherwise would be, because the university is 'egotistically' in love with its own drama and place in the drama of existence as great, high, a tower of excellence. This positions the student entering in without qualifications, seeking to be accredited as worthy by the university, as in a low place. Research tells us (e.g. Wilkinson and Pickett 2009) being low in a hierarchy is bad for your health. What do you think of this suggestion that the university, as full of drama, if at all you think it is, exacerbates student mental difficulties? That's pretty controversial. Not what universities want to think or feel about themselves.

Eli: Definitely. For sure. I think schools generally, I mean lower education K–12 schools also, make people ill. I think here you make a really insightful point in thinking about the university as a kind of height of the pyramid of the knowledge institutions. Where there is a sense of being in a higher-stakes environment, which magnifies or amplifies the ill-making effects of educational institutions. The basic practices of grading and exams rely on making students feel anxious and fearful about avoiding shame. That kind of everyday anxiety is heightened in universities. Students feel like it's even more high stakes for them, for their lives. The fear of becoming a dropout is also magnified in a university. You can imagine yourself as dropping from a higher height. The stigma of being a college dropout – you can imagine it as a very disgraceful kind of position in life. Mental illness in universities tends to be stigmatized. So it's hard to articulate those kinds of feelings when you have them and are feeling anxious or depressed.

Helen: There's a silence. That's at the heart of why I wanted to write this book in the first place. This sort of anger at the cheekiness of a university. I don't quite know how else to put it. Psychopathic? I think it's too strong. I don't think it's meant deliberately. I think it's just a blindness, an arrogance and an ignorance that they are behaving in a way which is a spiral of drama into which they draw people. They ask those people to pay an extortionate amount of money in order to get drawn into this drama triangle (see Karpman, 2014), where the student is instantly positioned as a victim of the system. The universities are persecutors. The students are paying for this. What kind of dynamic is that? They're paying to be stressed and paying to be in a low position, at risk of stigma, as you put it. As I put it, at risk of increased vulnerability to existing, inevitable fault-lines, that in a healthy environment might heal well enough.

If they dare to not conform or dare to say no and walk away, or, God forbid, be themselves through and through and refuse to perform the version that is 'acceptable' to and in the university, all that kind of thing. It makes people poorly, surely? All that. By that I mean inhabiting or coming to inhabit, as a consequence of being a university student, the full spectrum from moving towards being clinically ill, to finding themselves uncomfortable in their skin: dis-at-ease. Then the university slaps a bunch of stigma on it. It says, 'Oh, you're not making the grade. You're not good enough. You've got mental health problems, poor you, but vulnerable, inadequate, unsuitable you. Take some time out. In fact, perhaps you don't cut it here.' Does it do that? That, Eli, the idea of that dynamic makes me a bit annoyed. It's a package which one would laugh at if it wasn't so serious because *so many* people seem to be buying into it.

In this book we are talking in, I describe 'university fantasy' (see Chapter 2) as this crazy situation. Students are fantasizing about the university because the university PR and Marketing department is bigging up the experience. The life impact of attending a university, using false claims often about how fantastic the experience is going to be, how important for their life trajectory it's going to be. Then there is also the traditional societal *idea* of the university as a lofty and prestigious, aspirational pinnacle of learning. So students fantasize about a better life through university attendance, because our current world existence can really be quite a poor experience at times. For some, in general, and in some respects, we're surviving it the best we can. Life is always, at least, a bit of a struggle, right? So they go to the university as this sanctuary space, hoping for salvation from that struggle, for something brighter and higher. Which is another part of the drama triangle: that the university is the saviour, the rescuer of the victim of existence. The student enters in. Your contribution is helping me understand how that shift from the drama triangle situation could occur into a winner's triangle (see Choy 1990). Are you familiar with these triangles as a framework to understand and then handle productively and healthily otherwise negative dramatic scenarios?

Eli: No.

Helen: OK, so if I just briefly explain. Then if you could respond on your own terms? The book is trying to shift students from the drama triangle situation that they are inherently in on account of how the university behaves and on account of how the university doesn't take responsibility for the harm that it does. It would like to empower students to move into a position of winning. That's why it is called *Playing the University Game*. The winners' triangle position is that you state your vulnerability and take care of yourself. That would be to do a whole heap of self-care, on account of the stressful environment that one is picking up, whether you know it or not. Being compassionate to yourself as well, in this context of a situation where if you don't step up and perform, you're going to be a dropout or a failure or shameful. You need to find solutions to such positioning, not just accept it as a dynamic. That is possible to do. A winners' triangle approach is along these lines then of: (1) state your vulnerability and accept responsibility for your own part in the drama triangle occurring, (2) take care of yourself and then (3) compassionately but assertively seek solutions. Using that three-point plan, so to speak, you can move away from the three dramatic positions of being victim, rescuer or persecutor. Now I've briefly explained, how do you see university students owning a winners' triangle scenario in the context of a dramatic university?

Eli: Could you repeat that last part? Maybe I don't see that right. What's the triangle part of it?

Helen: Sorry, yes, I missed a step in explaining. You've got the three positions. First of the drama triangle. Then, hopefully of the winner's triangle, to follow, after the drama triangle has either occurred and done its dastardly work or as a precaution to not getting into the drama triangle in the first place. The positions in the drama triangle move constantly and they are: victim, persecutor and rescuer.

The two triangles contain different things. In the winner's triangle it is more attitudes to action rather than identities. A three-step programme of action: state your vulnerability and take responsibility, take care of yourself and assertively but not aggressively seek solutions. In the drama triangle the student can be a *victim* of the system – I think you inherently understand that position very well – where the university could be the *persecutor* by demanding the student perform according to certain criteria or else, but the student could shift and be the *persecutor* if the student seeks to complain about the university, thus the university can play the *victim*. I haven't seen much of that. Then there's the *rescuer* position where you're going to be rescuing someone from the *persecutor*. But the *rescuer* can shift and become a *victim* of the former *victim* who has changed role and is acting as a *persecutor*. The positions are not static at all. It is a cycle of destruction and despair. Which is why it's so vital an antidote be applied and if not already known, be found: the winners' triangle is just that. It works. It works *every* time. If applied well enough. To extricate oneself from negative drama. With time and patience. Although it takes some practice in the applying of it. We are constantly getting sucked into drama. People love drama. We live by it (see, e.g. Ang 1996; Cron 2012; Yorke 2014). Which is great if we are watching a film. Not so great if the action-change-thriller-horror-and-or-harm of a film is in some way affecting our personal life as real lived experience. Or shades of this.

It's feasible to suggest that if you, yourself Eli, are trying to save people from university drama you are a rescuer and you're still stuck in the drama. I mean, I totally agree with the ideas of your book. You know that. I think they are well conceived and fantastically presented (see Lees and Meyerhoff 2020). But I guess I'm very keen the students don't read a book like yours and think oh, 'woe is me! There's no hope then for me and the university!', right? Because that would be them stuck in the drama triangle as a victim of some aspect of the truth, but not realizing it. So to shift them to the winners' triangle, the students have to understand the vulnerability that would come from, say, reading your book. Or this one! If they got informed about the university by reading it, it would then be a case of preventing or extrapolating self from harm: owning what their part is, taking care of themselves, showing self-compassion, awareness of self, dealing with the situation in a realistic, bold way, entering into the university anyway, but with awareness as a solution and as a protector for self. Enjoying the good things too. Alongside this caring activity, you know, a full package of self-care includes appreciating what can be enjoyed. But seeking solutions to the anomalies and the crises points is important work as a student. Not just saying 'oh woe is me, I'm a victim, it's terrible here, the system is corrupt, nothing to be done, it all stinks' if that is how things are beginning to turn. They would seek to find their own way through. They can.

I don't believe for a minute the university will do that work for them, nor do I believe the university has a particular obligation or duty to guide the student through 100 per cent. It could help much more than it does by not enjoying its own position in a drama triangle so much and being more humble, aware of the feelings and insecurities and needs to overcome personal weaknesses of others presenting themselves to learn and self-develop. Truly strong in the moral sense it isn't (see Brennan and Magness 2019). Just a bit of a bully in being great, one could suggest. It could do more to allow students to orientate themselves in the culture, instead of the university system riding the culture like a horse; they are the master of the land, waving slightly from afar: like royalty. That's ridiculous. But it works for those already at the top, right? So students need to 'do it for themselves'. That's the subtitle of the book: *The Art of University-Based Self-Education*. That's the solution bit. How do you move through the university well and enjoy the process? How do you negotiate it without being in a drama triangle? And that's my question to you. It's a difficult question.

Eli: Yeah, it's a great question. There are a lot of parts to it. There are a lot of scripts or narratives that students and teachers and everybody who is associated with the university tend to subscribe to, that pull us into that drama triangle. I think a big challenge is how to get us to think critically about those narratives. To want to unsubscribe from them. In the first chapter of my book (Meyerhoff 2019) – the chapter after the introduction – I talked a bit about melodramatic and jeremiadic genres of narratives. I think this really relates to this kind of drama triangle. By believing in these kinds of stories[1] people remain stuck in that drama triangle or see themselves as actors in that drama triangle. I think such dramatic narratives are ones that we need to identify and we need to offer alternatives to them. I think those narratives, at their core, rely on the taken-for-granted narrative of the individual student rising up the levels of the education system. I talk about this as a kind of romance narrative with the individual overcoming obstacles along the way. He or she is a hero/heroine in the story of their own lives. They overcome obstacles in the education system and you can see each level – kindergarten through first, second, third, fourth grade – as a kind of personal obstacle to overcome. I think people, students, we, become habituated to believing in that romance narrative. That's a basic, behind-the-scenes, taken-for-granted narrative in our lives that pretty much everybody subscribes to. It's just become so institutionalized in practices of schooling and in the very infrastructure and built environment of schooling. Schools are built, even as buildings, in ways that segregate students into the grades and tracks within the grades. When we were young we were thrown into that infrastructure in schools. It's hard to disabuse ourselves of it, when it's so integral.

Helen: That climbing up to the top of the tower romance. Yes. Can I ask you just a specific question? I'm sorry to interrupt you, but it seems to me from what I've seen of American schools on television or in films, the kinds of dramatic narratives that are portrayed as the American schooling system, that romance is much stronger in America. This is ironic given in the United States there is a relatively huge economy, compared to other countries, of home educating. The high school narrative, you know the 'high school prom', 'high school graduation ceremony', all of these romantic things which make hardly any sense outside of America to be honest. What is that? It's very weird in some senses to a non-American, I could imagine. Certainly to me! I laugh at them internally. Are you all being brainwashed in America somehow with these powerfully identified rituals? I mean, what's going on?

Eli: It's really core to American identity. I think these rituals are a kind of a constant distraction from having knowledge about the fundamentally violent character of the American nation state. And of our complicity with that nation state as citizens. Particularly this idea of the American individual as self-made. That narrative is predicated on an ignorance about the violence of settler colonialism and white supremacist slavery that the American nation state is founded on. You can see that the construction of that self, the idea of the individualized, self-made, self-responsible subject – you can see that happening explicitly, if you look at education discourses that happened in boarding schools for Native American young people. There the idea of the self-made individual was portrayed in explicit contrast with the Indian as this kind of dependent figure whose dependence on the tribe was contrasted with the white individual, who was independent and could make themselves without relying on others. I'm giving this story as a way to think critically about the history behind the creation of this self that we take for granted today. We must look at the history of how those narratives of the self have become so taken for granted and institutionalized now. In the deeper history of it we can see more violent episodes, but the violence has been normalized as a background part of our everyday lives now.

Helen: That normalized background narrative is really shocking to an outsider to the American dream. Many of the films of American schools that I have watched show someone being shoved up against a locker, with a hand around their neck. Even Spiderman the good guy does it, for Pete's sake!, when he becomes the bad version 'Venom', that is. It's taken for granted that this is part of the ritual of the educational ladder: to rise above the bully you bully. If you can survive the bully somehow, then you're going to go up. If you can be the bully, you're already up. Nobody ever, it seems to me, is being held to account, having to take responsibility for the violence. It is framed as *the way*. In terms of the university and being an American student – one hopes this will sell itself as a book to be read by American university students – if they read it and they get what we're talking about, are they going to have some kind of nervous breakdown? That this way here is not about drama or forms of violence. We've opened up a whole Pandora's box of truth that they never got access to because of this strong brainwashing that goes on in your country? Or, are they just going to say 'What a load of foolish nonsense – these people are clearly deranged'? How stuck is it?

Eli: I think there's just so many different scripts or narratives that people subscribe to. It makes it pretty hard or almost impossible to get somebody to unsubscribe to all of them at once. I think it takes that kind of chip, chip, chipping away at the different layers of it all. Showing that there are different ways of thinking about the world, narrating the world, that people can subscribe to. To get them to change.

Helen: But it's not for us to get them to change, is it?

Eli: Well, I don't know. I guess it depends – depends on what – I don't know what. What are you thinking about?

Helen: My point there is if we're the ones who are getting them to change, we are the rescuers. We're still in the drama triangle. That's not a good place to be, to be talking about change. Because no change will occur. We are in your 'impasse', *stuck* in the drama triangle, cycling around the positions. All we can do is present a paradigm of understanding which somehow shocks them out of an old paradigm? Isn't that the only work that we can do? You know, it's to tell the truth and hope that they are interested. I mean, that's our hope, not because we're rescuers, but because we care about them, shall we say. Because of our own crisis points, our own anomalies and our own suffering. We've entered into a new paradigm and we think it's the better land, but we can't possibly drag anyone there. Someone once said the phrase to me 'You can drag a horse to water, but you can't make it drink.' I don't want actually to drag a horse to water either. I mean this is part of the philosophy of coercion and non-coercion in education. I don't want to drag a horse to water, but if I see that the horse needs water, otherwise it's going to suffer badly, well, I think it's my responsibility to attempt to drag it to the water if I know how to drag. Right? Or wrong? The horse is suffering. The equivalent here is writing a book that people can read if they wish, right? I put the book in front of them but I can't make them read. Unless they want to. Or speaking to you and having your perspective presented to them. Which because you are one of them, you're American. You understand their land, you understand their experience. You are saying something which is not on script – not part of the American script. They can take it or leave it. But it's good to have an alternative script to read if you are thirsty.

Eli: For me it's helpful to think about the limits of writing my book. Thinking about its purpose is to think about the limits of what is possible with the book as a kind of circulating material object. I think people rarely, if ever, change their minds or transform their way of seeing the world based on just reading a book alone. Books are often important parts of transformation. Yet, when we change or when a book has been affective, changing somebody's way of seeing the world, it's usually in a relationship with other people. Where it's read, they're reading it in the context of doing something with others. So maybe, for example, students might read our book or books and be involved in a student organizing project on their campus: like organizing for a freeze on tuition hikes or organizing to support undocumented migrant students at their university or supporting janitors at the university on strike, something like that. Having some kind of practical context where the words in the book resonate with some kind of collective practice that the reader is involved in – I think that allows the words to affect a person more powerfully.

Helen: That makes sense. Although I would say I'm slightly suspicious of the power of groups. On the one hand, groups are more powerful than individuals and yet on the other hand, groups are really difficult. I suppose there is that idea that a book is not the saviour of the person who, maybe, changes how they think or how they behave, because that would be very arrogant. That would be the same kind of arrogant white supremacy or missionary attitude that does harm in other domains, by assuming to be the saviour of those who are different. But any author of a book can't imagine that they are the agent of change, despite being the provider of an agent of change. The agent of change is an alchemy or a synthesis of the product of the book as an offering and the person who takes up the offering. Who self-educates by doing so. I was talking with my neighbour the other day and we ended up talking politics. An older guy – older people tend to have thought quite a lot, right? so they can be very thoughtful people – said, 'we need a solution, but there are no solutions.' We were talking about the state of the world. I said, 'I think there are solutions. I think I know of some solutions, but nobody's listening. So this work of solutions is to hope that people will listen and then maybe solutions can be called solutions. But until people actually open themselves to solutions or listen to solutions, there are no solutions.' In respect of your comment about there's the book, then there's the practical application of the ideas of the book in organizing for change, the suspicion I have is about people agreeing with each other in a group in order to organize against a common enemy. That is still in the drama triangle. That's not people listening. That's no solution. They are now persecuting the victim, who is the baddie. The baddie will eventually persecute those people for persecuting them. It will be a big drama. What's a solution about that? There must be another way, because this constant cycling around those positions of the drama triangle is not effective.

Eli: I think we can distinguish between what the self or subject looks like in the drama triangle compared to how subjectivity is shaped in alternative ways of seeking change in the world. In the drama triangle the self is seen as an independent, self-responsible entity, who is not a cause of the problem. That can be the rescuer positioned outside of the problem who can dictate a solution from a kind of external position. But there are no external positions here. The rescuer is part of the problem. They keep rescuing, thinking they are outside the problem, but they're not. That's how the cycle keeps perpetuating. An alternative mode of approaching the structural transformation of the world broadly would be to see that this self is implicated in the problem. The self, and our conception of the self, needs to transform along with the world.

Helen: How?

Eli: Through seeing the self as part of the world, and as made through interaction with the wider world, through collectives, engagement with others, other people and things in the world. Then, recognizing that the problems we see in the world also infuse our own selves. In grappling with changing the world we also need to grapple with changing ourselves. This is a coterminous and interweaved process of changing the world and changing ourselves at the same time. It's a messier process, that doesn't lend itself to simplified narratives of drama.

Helen: That's why I reacted to your book the way I did, is it not (see Lees and Meyerhoff 2020)? I think your book went straight into me in such a profound way, that I'm barely cognizant of how much it dovetails with what I was already thinking. Almost gives the framework. I've been looking at this drama triangle/winners' triangle thing for about three years. Your book is a model of the drama triangle entering into the winner's triangle. It's just you didn't know that theory, surely? You said that you see that it's the same framework. I found it very interesting because it was messy towards the solutions part at the end, because it was difficult, because it wasn't the solution, the rescuer package. Even research at university is always offering the rescuer position: here's the problem and research solves the problem or part of it, really nicely and everything is going to be OK – right now with the Covid vaccine, this is the saviour of the world, and so on. But that's not the whole truth. Is it? We know that there will be another pandemic down the road, according to the research and the commentators, because of the way that the environment has been abused. The vaccine doesn't help with that. It delays the solution which is to pay attention on a much wider scale to the harm done to the environment and to listen to nature, each other, about a way forward. To take responsibility for the harm we've done and indeed continue to do so and to stop it in light of that responsible vision. In that sense, a university student who is hoping, seeking, they read my book, they read your book, they read *a* book, they join a university union or movement or something and they're gonna end up with a much better world, a much better position. It's just not true. There is a long journey ahead, involving *taking account* of oneself. That's hard.

What hope then can we offer them for a smile? You know the book was originally called *Enjoy Yourself*. What's the good news, Eli?

Eli: Well, I don't know. I'm not totally pessimistic about the possibilities for people to make change. To make the world a better place. I think change happens in collaboration with others. In broad, broad movements. I think people every day are themselves making their world, in at least a microcosm, change towards a better way. During the pandemic which began in 2020, people have been taking care of each other in their neighbourhoods, on their blocks, when their governments are failing them. They are voluntarily cooperating with each other, giving each other mutual aid. Families are taking care of each other right now, but also going beyond the bounds of biological family to help each other out on a neighbourhood level and across cities. I think those kinds of grassroots practices of helping each other can be the basis for broader transformations of our world. The problem is that we keep relying on university-trained experts to come in and offer solutions from above. Those solutions tend to just perpetuate the underlying deeper, systemic problems with our world. If we stop believing in the saviours, the rescuers from above, and instead study with each other in more grassroots practices of helping each other, we can build from those grassroots practices, to effect broader scale changes.

Helen: Well, I'll leave you there. Your day is very precious, I understand that. Thank you very much for your time. If I could just end with one comment, which is that you have positioned the university and the students' experience as something which can be fruitful, beneficial, enjoyable, if the student, instead of competing with their fellow students, embraces the community of the student and works with them in a collaborative, communicative, cooperative way. Then that, does it not, makes the university a good place in lieu of any other situation. Have I understood you correctly?

Eli: Yes. I think at a fundamental level that ideal of student cooperation offers an alternative to the norm of students competing with each other and feeling anxious and ashamed and being positioned as victims. At a basic level cooperative, collaborative practices could be a start for making the university a better place.

2

The Rules of the University Game

As previously mentioned this book is not a definitive guide to anything, because particular guidance for anything can only come from you and your unique self and circumstances. You know best. However, there are some core issues about being in a university to which we can attach some useful ideas. Given this book is framed as about a game I have called them 'rules'. Nevertheless, the game we are discussing in this book is not like this: 'one cannot (really) win the game unless one plays it, and one cannot (really) play the game unless one obeys the rules of the game' (Suits 1978: 24). Why? Because, first, going to or being in a university in whatever way or for whatever reason is part of human experience. There is a profoundly important sense in which our lives and experiences are not a game but something much more sensitive and meaningful. Our lives are not reducible to gaming 'metanarratives' and about any of these we are entitled to be incredulous (Lyotard 1984). Second, we are inventing a new 'game' and, in doing so, it isn't a game anymore because that is *our* game; it's a life of university experience lived as well as possible. What follows in this chapter are some thoughts to consider that might be helpful (rather than gaming rules) and that is different from 'rules of the game'. The university game, then, has no 'family resemblance' (Wittgenstein 1992: N° 67) to playing, being played or being in or part of a game of any kind. Except that possibly *lovingly* devised by a holy force, whatever game/s (as such) a holy force might play (with this being only relevant to those who might believe in a holy force in the first place), or indeed, games which are up for deconstruction by their very nature such as writing and its reception (see, e.g. Lyotard 1985). So our game ought to have a new word or phrase to describe it. If I have to choose I would say 'seeking place and direction in the world and in self' (amid difficult and challenging factors) or 'the attempt to maintain an abiding awareness of Self' in the sense of Internal Family Systems (Earley 2009;

Schwartz 2021). There are many other approaches that promote our being centred in a sense of ourselves that is grounding, this being a direction to which we can look if we trust education is a good thing. Amid interesting debates about games and what they are, can we acknowledge the 'university game' (*their* game) is a game with a resemblance to poker? A bit like chess? Does it offer a taste of white-water rafting? Or archery? We acknowledge this possibility based on experiences and stories told. So, involved as we are in university spaces, knowing (whatever knowing might mean) about their game – and *our* rules to play and win – is here recognized as helpful.

Rule 1: Autonomy Matters

A student entering into university study or a staff member taking up a new university post is entering into institutional life. An institution is, frankly, a system. It relies on you behaving yourself and adhering to its protocols for what you say, do and even think: '[university] students [and staff] are summoned to adjust their behaviour and learning to fit with culturally implicit norms and pedagogical demands. To be legitimated and rewarded is to inhabit and perform requisite skills and roles' (Wilkins and Burke 2015: 434). Being systematically 'acceptable', not spontaneous nor quirky, is what counts. It's how you count. But, is that good for you? Should you be *accidentally* acceptable by nature to the system, my thought is that you ought to enjoy your relaxed luck. Yet, if you have an *other* nature, don't lose it. Stand firm for it. This is, in both cases, autonomy. An example of how, sadly, I didn't do that was when I lost my childhood Essex accent (which has a London East End gruffness to it) to speak 'posh' at a university full of privileged students schooled in an 'upper' class accent. I panicked, I guess, because I felt so 'wrong' and like an outsider to what was a system of how to be. You will have your own examples of such challenges. Another example of standing firm, that applies more at the level of epistemology and ways to think about things, is if *you* think a certain way – valuing the ways of women for example (Belenky et al. 1997) or *value* the presentation of a certain cultural heritage (Gutiérrez y Muhs et al. 2012). Universities work primarily through a dominant white, patriarchal, colonial perspective (Lloyd 1984; Kauffman and Perry 1989; Peters 2019) and are significantly run by men: 'I continue to observe decision-makers often thinking of men first, or only of men, when searching for suitable leadership candidates' (Devlin March 7 2021). So, thinking like a women or an Indigenous medicine healer is going to be foreign and even weird in the university system. That's a shame. Whoever you are, to maintain your autonomy to be yourself is to hold tight to the preciousness of what and who you are. It is to not acquiesce to releasing your hold on this in a university space of time and place because of systemic forces from outside yourself that might suggest you don't quite fit.

Signs of subversion and diversion from the following of an institutional script that legitimates a person are very often seen as threatening by those within that institution and system who have 'obeyed'. Obedience to the norms and rules of others and to the group is often, although not always, done out of forms of fear. This is reason number one why autonomy matters: it means you haven't lost yourself and you are unafraid of dangerous group-think. You maintain your individuality. This is sanity. It's also autonomy as an educational approach. In a university to unfollow a 'group-agreed' script at the academic level and having a perspective autonomous from a standardized way of thinking about any given focus for writing can be an excellent thing. It's called originality. It's what works to win academic prizes and prestige in the form of pleasing relative results of some kind: otherwise known as good marks or interest in your thinking. However, for an original thesis or contribution to function as a good thing in a university it needs to be informed by all that surrounds it. Other intellectual contributions matter, including group-think with which you may not agree. You need to have as solid as possible a foundation of knowing and acknowledging (which is to cite relevant literature) of what has already been said. So, in this sense, you are far from autonomous from the 'canon' and its friends (other work that cites the canon and relates to your writing) but you can approach it as your own producer: 'Autonomy does not frighten winners' (James and Jongeward 1971: 2) and 'student-as-producer' is an exciting new way for universities to relate to and with students which privileges their voice over given scripts (Neary 2016; Neary and Winn 2016). To be autonomous is to tread your own intellectual path while being aware of the path others have taken.

Because in places like universities there are rules of power, it is important for your mental well-being to not feel powerless despite your probable low place in a mirage of hierarchy. The university rules of power find themselves most obviously expressed in hierarchies. There are plenty of those in universities – student bodies, academic and administrative staff and of course managers all fit into ladders of power. While hierarchies as power play are childish nonsense, you need to sort of pretend to care about them in order to not ruffle feathers. You ought not to kowtow (be obsequious) but you ought to keep quiet about your profound and righteous lack of respect for puffed-up egos who think they are someone bigger and better than you. Silence can serve you. This is to play well in the university game for the game is saturated by hierarchies you need to navigate. Channel an internal vision of Super Mario Bros and have some fun.

Sometimes it is entirely possible that you might genuinely admire and respect someone for who they are or what they do in terms of university life.

A professor whose work you admire? No problem. Scott (1990) asks, 'How do we study power relations when the powerless are often obliged to adopt a strategic pose in the presence of the powerful and when the powerful may have an interest in overdramatizing their reputation and mastery' (xii)? There is a nice relationality in your so-called powerlessness and admiring someone who does not overdramatize their position. It's called curiosity. Curiosity is good. You do need to *protect* yourself against those with power who do not care about the effects of their actions on you, by being aware of their moves. Their puffiness. See the next rule.

Your autonomy from the system and its protocols or rules of who and how to be need to be presented carefully. Writing and informed academic opinions are the very best way to do that: on the stage of scholarly interactions. Outside of the academic frame but remaining within universities for social life I suggest you just be yourself and be joyful, proud and relaxed about doing so. See my foregoing comments about forces from without and the danger of losing yourself to a system's demands upon you personally. Autonomy, so strange to schooled societies, is a wonderful thing and is extremely good for a robustly healthy sense of self (Goodsman 1992; Sheffer 1995; Thomas and Pattison 2007; Lees 2011). It takes work to be autonomous in universities: educational pride, courage and boldness, as well as personal love of self, as is.

If autonomy is a foreign concept – and that's not your fault but the fault of something called a school system (Bowles and Gintis 1976; Willis 1981) – then be of good cheer because one of the most vital roles a university can have is to foster autonomy. Ironic? Rather. Nevertheless it's true that universities are idiosyncratic, self-contradicting entities. In this department of 'value for money' make sure you get the product.

There is a caveat to all this autonomy-freedom-and-relax chat. As a student you are in the matrix of the university on account of your dependency on the university for your desired qualification or other outcome. I assume you want the qualification you signed up for and are technically paying for, all being well with your standard of writing. What if you don't play by their rules? It is possible that the result will be large or small forms of 'educational trauma' (Gray 2019), which is an actual thing, as is what I call 'educationism' – the prejudice against other, possibly preferred, ways of doing education and learning (Lees 2015). Said differently: it is slightly their way or the highway. If the university is the power and the pedagogy at the intellectual level – and this can happen if you encounter a reviewer-marker who sees your work as too far outside acceptability for reasons of difference (rather than incompetence) – then you need to deal with this. The way to do so is to have read a lot of relevant literature. Be smartly different and defended by scholarship, not just otherwise opinionated. You can say almost anything in a university setting (bar advocating hate or harm) if you have a good and secure argument, anchored in literature. It's called being convincing. There is no need to be 'right' because right is relative and therefore unreliable for some.

Universities place you, sift you, label you, determine the value of you. You signed up for it. The key is to not be hurt by the standards or the judgements. To not believe them very much. This would be to maintain your autonomy from the system and its 'binaries'. What I'm essentially saying, in so many different ways, is believe in yourself in the face of the university's forms of power. The way to do that is not believe the university is more wonderful or more powerful than you. It isn't. Why? Because it doesn't have a heart.

Rule 2: Find Out What It Says in Black and White

I didn't know the rules of the game when I was an undergraduate, and silences were everywhere. No one was telling me how to play. For example, no one told me *to read*. I wish they had done so because it would have been a useful first interaction for me, given my background. That was an important missing instruction for my capacity in my undergraduate discipline of philosophy and I'm still in recovery, playing catch-up for lost reading others dived into, knowing somehow what I had never be guided to understand. We make our way somehow? Find out what the *key* instructions of what to do to win are for your discipline and do not fail to follow those instructions. There are likely just a couple you cannot do well without. Reading is one. Thinking is another. These instructions will be often implicit, tacit or quietly known and assumed. Possibly even passed along chains of friendship or collegiality. While you might encounter that quiet transferring of knowledge, you can bet they are written down somewhere as well. This is a university! Universities write what they are in order to exist. Search for instructions and see the previous rule.

An instruction I can give you in black and white here that will not let you down is get to know the library. I missed the library tour because I was having a chat with new friends, which was one example in a catalogue of errors as an undergraduate. There were others. I missed essay help sessions because I hadn't read the departmental board for news. I lacked understanding of the essay grading schema and had no idea for which standards or content types I was aiming in writing. I didn't know what I could or should expect from the course. Don't be like that. Pay attention to the university brochure promises and chase up the promised products: libraries, sports facilities, help sessions. Whatever it is, if you see it written down search for it as a material fact. Expect delivery as a result of your search based on writing seen and digested, because that is how the game at university works. Read the university handbook or other literature handed to you, including timetables, deadlines, course requirements, reading lists, library protocols for attaining books (for there are many types of borrowing and some books get taken out by the clued-up students quickly). Most of all read the grading scheme for your discipline and study level: this tells you what mark you can expect for what types of presentation in your writing or other submissions for assessment. Also, survey the campus map. Orient yourself well so you can flow around the space. This will save you time and help you feel in control.

Pay close attention to anything written down in black and white, either on paper or online because ignorance can bite. Why am I emphasizing writing in a university? Because everything *functions*, for good and for bad, in a university through writing. Your rights. Your experience. Their expectations and demands of you. Their chance to deal with you as they see fit. Their adjudications and the award of your grades. That is why staff at universities attend horrible, endless committee meetings. Because if it isn't written down it doesn't touch you and at committee meetings what gets written down gets decided. Often stealthily. So pay attention. Universities are good at covering their backs and even have legal experts to assure that back is covered. Backs get covered if it's written down. Remember that when you email someone in a university. Universities have and use surveillance: of emails and in other ways, including many, many CCTV cameras. Don't forget your email account and its contents are their property. It's not your email account and it definitely isn't private. Be careful what you commit to writing and share within the university matrix that isn't part of the care of writing for scholarly activities. Think about joining the student union so you can influence the mechanisms of writing that might affect you and other students.

So that's the easy bit. The knowable and hold-them-and-you-to-account written code bit. Alas, there is another kind of code. It isn't in black and white on a page, more a thousand shades of grey colouring the sky above you. As an academic working in universities I've seen students suffer from the same kind of ignorance I had during both my undergraduate and postgraduate degrees about a university's 'culturally implicit norms' (Wilkins and Burke 2015: 434). I've also seen staff suffer. There is a generalized 'L plate' lack of clue-ness about what is expected and how to behave or *be* (an italic which sends a shudder up my spine – see my comments about violence). It's a struggle for me to mention these norms because I find them so rude; so despicable. As you might already be able to tell I don't agree with their coercive power to attempt you to get you to hand over your autonomy, your individual sovereignty in exchange for acceptance and being acceptable. But those norms are dangerous to ignore, even if ignoring what you see and discover is then exactly what you choose to do. If you aren't reading a book like this how do you find out the game to be played beyond what you've heard on the grapevine, seen on the TV and in movies and sensed vaguely so far about universities? You'd be lost *while* you were becoming lost to yourself. Is this part of why there is significant mental distress among students?: 'Levels of mental illness, mental distress and low wellbeing among students in higher education in the UK are increasing, and are high relative to other sections of the population' (Thorley 2017: 3–4). I hope what is written down in *this* black-and-white document can help with navigation and staying at the helm or wheel of your personal transport through the silent, unwritten experiential land and sea of universities. Keep a compass to hand.

Rule 3: Be Polite and Respectful

Academia ought to be a polite, respectful environment because disagreeing matters and is necessary. Gentle manners in interaction go a long way to having great conversations and making true and wonderful connections with others, especially when part of the task is disagreeing.

Rule 4: Breathe!

The best thing you can do for yourself there, then, now and in the future is to breathe deeply. Given there is much to agitate you and more than enough to consciously or subconsciously cause you to feel anxiety, your key and free weapon of choice should be your breathing. Breathe deeply and slowly: in-breath for energy and release from feeling frozen with fear or anxiety, out-breath for reclaiming calm. This helps to connect healthily with the polyvagal system and regulate you (Culver 2021). Why breathing with awareness? Because the science is clear: it will help you educationally and personally cope with what you are encountering in university spaces and paces as stress, fear, anxiety (Nhat Hanh 1990; Patten 1997; Erricker and Erricker 2001; Orr 2002; Zembylas and Michaelides 2004; Kabat-Zinn 2005; Ollin 2008; Huppert and Johnson 2010; Lees 2012; Orr 2012). It also induces pleasant feelings. Pick some form of meditative-mindful practice and stick with it. These practices are very helpful in education (Lees 2012) and not just there. They are a true boon to a thriving life.

Rule 5: University Fantasizing Is a Mistake

It's not sexual and it's not sexy to fantasize about the university. It's just wrong. I don't mean in the moral sense. It's wrong because it will harm you. The power and the prestige of universities is somewhat sexy, sometimes, but in general it is a mistake to engage with that glamorous mirage: 'The prime responsibility is to insist on the distinction between truth and untruth, verifiable belief and wishful thinking, fact and fantasy' (Gibbs and Peterson 2019: 9). As many have commented, fantasizing about the university is common (Craig 2018) or being led to fantasize, based on marketing spin, which is something else (Svensson and Wood 2007). Being spun a tale about how *greeeaaat* a university is for you is increasingly an issue because not all claims exiting university PR offices are true. Even the university itself fantasizes about how *greeeeeaaat* it is, when it isn't exactly (Ellen 2017; Brennan and Magness 2019): 'Every managerial university now puts out a cloud of imagery, text and sound intended to misrepresent the way things really are' (Connell 2019: 131).

It is a social fantasy that we all ought to go to university if we want to *be* someone. The perpetuation of this myth hurts some people who might just be far happier and better off making boats or cutting hair, both fine and useful professions likely not needing a university degree but instead years of practical, technical experience on the job and apprenticeship (Watts and Bridges 2006). An agenda known as the 'widening participation' agenda (or similar names such as 'universal participation', see Cahalan 2013) means, just like with people believing it is compulsory to attend a school, when it is very often and mostly not (Lees 2013a) and 'good' to do so, when it is inherently not (Goodman 1971; Gatto 1992; Flint and Peim 2012; Peim 2012), the university has managed to pose as the poster child for great things, great futures, greatness. Fantasy land.

Let's talk about infrastructure: buildings, resources. Yes, universities have nice buildings. Many have a lot of money; some billions in endowments (Brennan and Magness 2019). Some are ancient and look pretty. Something to dream about like punting down the river? Lovely. Wrapping a stripey, multi-coloured scarf around your neck? Cool. Universities have clubs, societies, bars, cafes, libraries, hefty infrastructure, or at least some do. The social network of a university is substantial. Fantasizing about making great friends or meeting the eyes of one's future partner across a crowded lecture theatre, bumping into said desired person in a medieval lane or a minimalist departmental foyer, or accidentally brushing against their leg with long-lasting consequences in a seminar event, are all possible in this prestigious infrastructure. Do you trust yourself and your mind and your welfare as a person in development to infrastructure?

Rule 6: Be Aware of University Fear and Consent to Not Know

Students will each feel fear differently, in differing quantities, for differing reasons and on different occasions. Fear is part of university experience. If you, like me, have experienced fear when it comes to academic study, occasions, dynamics, silences, it may be that the primary source of fear is of not knowing how or what to do. This is what I call 'university fear'. We can also call it stress at meeting a task of which you feel incapable. How to write the essay? What to write in the essay? How to get a good grade? How to behave to be acceptable in a university gathering? What to say? How to say it? What not to say? How not to say it? What to wear, what not to wear, what look fits in, what look to avoid? What attitude to hold and show or not show? The fear that circles like a vulture around, above, these unknowns is a real stress with physiological impacts that – as a cumulative pile of considerations – can detrimentally affect your health. It's not exactly a picture of relaxed joy for most people. While you can ease into it, the very fact that people might approach their first encounters with universities fearfully tells us quite a lot about the environment.

In a university, given the busyness with which those employed by the university lead their university lives, if you are pausing, stopping to reflect, admitting fear and other responses to feeling afraid of aspects of being in a university, then alas you may be without help. I found throughout my university experiences that fear of the university itself as culture or idea was the silent observer, the unspoken element. Most people seemed to me to be afraid of something, someone, some silence they couldn't quite nail. No one talked about it, of course. Perhaps those brave and wise enough to attend counselling sessions spoke of it, or they moaned about it at home to release tension, but mostly it struck me that fear circulated, wild, untamed, on campuses and beyond, in cyber campuses. I didn't like that much. I expect neither do you, if you agree with me about fear being silently ubiquitous in universities. Research suggests fear has a strong correlation with stress and anxiety, although fear is for threats known and anxiety for the vaguely sensed:

> For some authors, fear and anxiety are undistinguishable, whereas others believe that they are distinct phenomena. . . . Many authors, however, have argued that differences in their etiologies, response patterns, time courses, and intensities seem to justify a clear distinction between anxiety and fear. Although both are alerting signals, they appear to prepare the body for different actions. Anxiety is a generalized response to an unknown threat or internal conflict, whereas fear is focused on known external danger. (Steimer 2002: 233)

In the case of being at a university the irony is that the known external danger is of not knowing, of possibly failing to meet a standard and of being judged to be deficient. To allow that to hit you is a choice. You need to consent to not know which is to face the fear and embrace it healthily. Agree that not knowing is a part of it all. This consent also, if the above quote is to be useful, might help you deal with the anxiety of the unknown. Embrace the darkness through an autonomous choice and see it as pure adventure?

If this is you, the afraid student, take a moment and be kind to yourself because it isn't your fault. You are not to blame. It isn't right nor proper that university fear and vulnerability might be a significant element of your experience. See the next rule about not knowing and its antidote.

Rule 7: Want to Know

The antidote to university fear is consent and curiosity, which Chen mentions in the conversation later as a key qualification of being a student and being the right kind of student to enjoy yourself. Curiosity is autonomous exploration within a kind of education where people flourish because their autonomy is encouraged (Lees and Noddings 2016). Despite coercive aspects of university life as a hidden curriculum, universities *do* encourage scholarly autonomy: it's a part of their profile and 'manners'. It sounds coercive of me to insist you be curious. After all you are paying for university time so why *should* you be curious? Quite simply, if you aren't you will have nothing to say in your writing that is stimulating for the reader. The deal is that you engage fully with wanting to know and it will protect you: in essay writing, debating, researching, social interactions. Wanting to know is not a possession of some kind of elite species of university attender but instead the attitude that a student rightly arrives with and demands as an atmosphere: you want to know and you expect – for your fee paid and/or your life sacrifices endured – that your desire to know will be accommodated. Given universities are machines to 'play with ideas' (Labaree 2017: 190), you might be in luck. You've come to the right place.

Rule 8: Do Not Play in a University Drama Unless You Are Acting with the Drama Society

This is when you suffer, whether you are on top flying high, down and dependent, or running to help. University drama in action is not, in this sense, when the student theatre group is putting on a great show. It's when things become intense. Intense experiences involve drama (Karpman 1968: 1). The university drama is being played out in two ways, or on two levels, each of which hit your experience: institutional and personal.

Rule 8 is about the institutional drama: 'shifts and transformations that have occurred at both individual and structural levels in higher education during the last three decades' (Ergül and Coşar 2017: 7); 'changes in the labour processes of academic work (Smyth 1995), have also dramatically changed the nature of knowledge creation and utilization in universities' (Smyth 2018: 36); 'Since 2000 there have been dramatic changes in the nature of higher education' (Biggs and Tang 2011: 3); '*enormous* increases in [student] borrowing' (Nelson and Watts 1999: 105–7, emphasis in the original); 'It is a no-brainer, that universities everywhere are experiencing unprecedented changes. . . . This is not a recipe for a robust and vibrant university system' (Smyth 2018: v); 'about ten thousand students, with African American torch bearers leading the way, walked in the cold from the university to the capitol in the largest student march of the Black Campus Movement (BCM)'. (Rogers 2012: 1); 'the noisy scenes of protest . . . severe tuition hikes . . . means that police officers and other law enforcement agents are in full gear and out in full force' (Chatterjee and Maira 2014: 1);

> For some time now, universities have been described as corporations, 'unscrupulous profiteers', and 'system[s] out of control' (Bok 2004; Bousquet 2008; Mettler 2014) that are 'exacerbating' and 'perpetuating' inequality and a 'caste system' (Guinier 2015; Mettler 2014; Stevens 2007) by 'laundering privilege' (Stevens 2007: 248). It is a system where academics either practice 'barbaric rituals' (Bolaño 2004), or, as part of the growing legion of part-timers and adjuncts, are flushed out like 'waste'. (Bousquet 2008; O'Sullivan 2016: 1)

I haven't covered any of these issues in any depth, and putting each dramatic 'scene' in context isn't part of the point. What matters is realizing how very much embedded the university is in the weft and weave of drama playing itself out in the short and long term. How it was and will be thus enmeshed in so many ways and for complex historical reasons (Labaree 2017; Brennan and Magness 2019; Peters 2019) that include the reality of recent exponential growth and increased business (not educational) modelling connected to growth's financial incomes (Collini 2017). Students enter this arena when they sign up for a course of study. While you may consider your progress happily through your studies without institutional and political drama affecting or touching your experience, this is unlikely. The touch may seem to be from afar, a view only or something heard, but the drama will be ever present around you. If it does touch you, as a student you possibly may not have the vocabulary to name it and call it out, especially at first. Perhaps neither will some staff if they believe at all in universities as innocent ivory towers of intellectual delight. I hope the conversations in this book go some way to helping with orientation. Remember the compass to keep yourself safe.

I haven't included any particular quotes here about the issues of sexism, sexual harassment, police on campus, local area troubles (for instance at Oxford where the city lives in the shadow of its famous university), plagiarism, essay mills, classism, elitism, bullying, mobbing, zero-hours or fixed-term contracts and the effects of this on student experience and value for money or on staff experience. It's a fact that there are academic superstars (Nelson 1997; Smyth 2018), pension crises causing strikes and the downsizing of departments to make up shortfalls in budgets. Despite the growth and income just mentioned universities are themselves vulnerable to the 'weather'. We can ask: 'What will Covid do?' for example. I could get into all these problems. It would be another book entirely were we to dwell on these issues. This isn't a book about university drama. It's a book about how to avoid it.

Rule 9: Do Not Get Stuck in Personally Affecting Drama Triangles

There is also the personal drama of university life. As Smyth says: 'There is a conspicuous absence of studies that give existential accounts of what life is like for students in the contemporary university' (2018: vii). An absence of studies is where we need to focus on people's personal life when and even because they are living within a university atmosphere. Universities are dramatically dangerous places for stress (Lew et al. 2019; McCloud and Bann 2019; Morrish 2019). If we find ourselves in a calm environment it's rather easy to be, ourselves, calm. If we are, however, in today's universities, how does that affect us? If staff aren't safe to speak and neither are students what happens? The answer is disconcerting, intense pressure (see Morrish 2017, 2019). Pressure of this kind isn't sexy and it isn't cool. It's a problem. Instead of facing problems democratically, robustly, maturely, universities are using gag orders to silence dissenting staff when they leave the academy (Parr 2014; Havergal 2019; Anonymous 2021; Geoghegan 2021; Ross 2021). They also use such gagging practices to silence students who take up an issue with a university. Eggshells, anyone? Such an atmosphere is a student issue.

Drama triangles of victim, persecutor or rescuer (Karpman 1968, 2007; McKimm and Forrest 2010; Gerlock 2012) are rife in universities. When this is silent, silenced, shameful to discuss, peppered with fees payment and debt issues and sandwiched between slices of university fantasy-desire, the meal is poison. It is then no wonder student mental health is undeniably challenged, as this counselling survey shows: 'Anxiety continues to be the most predominant presenting concern among college students (41.6%), followed by depression (36.4%), and relationship problems (35.8%)' (Mistler et al. 2012: 5).

Are all these students covered by that survey just mentioned so socially inept, weak and troubled they cannot cope with higher education? It helps *a lot*, whatever the degree of distress a person is going through, if students are in an environment of non-dramatic care and educational attention. But universities exacerbate drama. They manage themselves through drama. It's the management style and it's the control mechanism (Fleming 2021). Voice? Not really. For that you need a union representative or a lawyer by your side.

In the university so many crumble and despair. Resilience factors are shredded. Is the university affecting students at the level of their own, natural and normal background personal drama and making it worse? An education should not harm and stunt you. It should heal you and help you to grow into health, through the benefits of an education. Context of culture, place and atmosphere is vital to take account of in education. It matters. It is part of an education and highly influential.

If we consider the same survey of students mentioned earlier in this chapter, but seven years later, the problems are not being resolved and getting better, but are getting worse: '87.3% of directors reported experiencing an increased demand for counseling services in the past year' (LeViness et al. 2019: 1). So is it challenging for universities and *for students and their families and friends* that students are in a university? If it is, games being played are not being played with well-being in mind. They are just being played and without enough care.

Not all students and staff find it extremely challenging but I wonder if you will or do experience challenge where there ought to be study, curiosity, thinking, flourishing and calm. This seems a drama too far:

> In the UK, the All Party Parliamentary Group on Students – a forum established for MPs and their peers to discuss issues that affect students in higher education – found 33% of students had experienced suicidal thoughts in the past academic year. (Gorczynski 2018)

They're kidding, right? A third of students in one of the most apparently prestigious higher education countries in the world think about ending their lives? That isn't normal. Presenting this data outside of its academic context is to miss a great deal of the complexity involved in such a shocking finding. However, we can tell one thing from such reporting: there is a problem, Houston, and the problem is NASA, not the rocket:

> It has been clear for some time that the higher education student body has experienced a decline in mental health. The Guardian has highlighted a sharp rise in students requesting counselling services. In this environment,

new interventions have become acutely necessary and there is now a charity, Student Minds, dedicated to improving student mental health. In June 2018, Sam Gyimah, then the Minister for Universities, Science, Research and Innovation, proposed a student mental health charter for universities. In March 2019, there was an announcement of a new student mental health taskforce. (Morrish 2019: 13)

Personal drama. Being at university should be good for you, in every way, by design and with attention, without particular exception or deviation. There should be no neglect of a possibility that being a student can *hurt* you. Being an academic means you get paid to get ill in a toxic environment. Not ideal but – being a student would mean *you pay* to get ill.

Rule 10: Personally Stay in the Winner's Triangle

It is important to enjoy university. To get free of drama – get drama vaccinated. If you desire to attend a university, one needs to understand what is occurring structurally in your experience. Karpman's 'drama triangle' theory is cited earlier. This framework exposes the dramatic dynamics brilliantly and you need to recognize the drama before you can escape it: 'Drama compares to transactional games, but drama has a greater number of events, a greater number of switches per event, and one person often plays two or three roles at once' (Karpman 1968: 2). These events and switches involve time seemingly speeding up and breathing increasing as stress elevates (see rule 4). Relational and educational dynamics can go wrong if you cannot pause (Rowe 1974; Lees 2013b). The roles of victim, persecutor and rescuer Karpman mentions (Karpman 1968) in such enmeshed, fast-paced, inexorable gaming are none of them helpful.

A wonderful characteristic of academic study is that it affects your mind in ways that help you rise above the everyday. This rising up mentally is to ride on ideas, and it is good fun. You will not get to that space of personal interest unless you get free of drama. You will struggle with studentship and scholarship and be susceptible to dramatic diversions in the lacuna where calm, curious, clear-headed, confident, connected, compassionate, courageous, creative (Earley 2009; Schwartz 2021) success ought to be. It helps if you get past the illusion of the university as a fantasy object that will 'do' studentship for you (see rule 7). This is to turn on, like a light, your own interests. This is a move into self-educating and taking responsibility for yourself in the context of a game. It is to move into the winner's triangle and out of the drama triangle. Choy outlines, with an antidote to Karpman's 'drama triangle' of victim, persecutor and rescuer, a 'winner's triangle' of being vulnerable, assertive and caring (Choy 1990). She states, 'The Winner's Triangle . . . allows the subject to function autonomously.' I suggest it can also work the other way around: if we function autonomously (see rule 1), we can get into the winner's triangle. A 2012 study of online learning communities has relevance for us because the issue of note in the study was 'relational challenges'. Gerlock (2012) found an organic and interrelating process was occurring between self-regulated learning in students and diminution of negative drama triangle circling: students who learned in a self-educated way were involved in less drama. Crucially, to take control by self-educating is to set your own pace and this is to slow down dramatic role switching so you can call it out should it occur. In going 'existentially' slower you can take time to acknowledge any vulnerabilities, voice assertively your needs and show yourself due care.

All of this go-at-your-pace-control (instead of being in a whirl of drama) gives a sense of oneself and it is a sense of self achieved through this type of self-led education (Goodsman 1992; Greenberg and Sadofsky 1992; Sheffer 1995; Thomas and Pattison 2007, 2013; Lees 2018). This sense operates healthily in the context of the world which is what a university-level education can and should do for you. Taking control of your education also enables inter-relationality and good enough approaches to teaching and learning (Bingham 2008), meaning you don't expect your teachers to deliver perfect content that you 'consume' – instead they are facilitators *of your own agenda*. Students can put teaching and learning in a context of acceptance, curiosity and personal inquiry, rather than customer dissatisfaction. Through controlling how you approach studying at the personal level of deciding, acting autonomously and enjoying the various freedoms involved in university spaces as a student in these otherwise dramatic environments, you can find your flow. The oil to apply to avoid tension and dramatic log-jams in your experience is self-education (see all rules presented in this chapter). The conversations in this book are all designed to give you a sense of what self-education means in university life.

Rule 11: Use the University and Enjoy Yourself

I'll keep this brief because not much needs to be said: use the university like it uses you. It uses you to make up numbers, to supply tuition fee money, to pay for the accommodation services it runs and to contribute financially to various other areas of the income column in the budget, like teaching and administration. It uses that you show up. It uses you to be a university. It uses you to contribute to the making of a dynamic community. THIS is the university - you: *universitas magistrorum et scholarium* – a world of teachers and students. It is yours to use and squeeze and ride and bellow through with grace and joy. Don't forget that, while you are there, you own it. Treat it kindly. Expect it will treat you well and be clear and calm when it does not. Seek solutions in the face of any discrepancies to the deal. Above all use it to serve you as a self-reliant student who educates themselves, using the myriad facilities for which you pay. Enjoy your books, your friendships, your discussions, your drama-free university education. This is a rule.

3

What Kind of Student Will You Be?

This conversation with Pat is part of the building up for students in this book of successful strategies to succeed and flourish in universities. Pat is a stalwart refusnik of the thoughtless and unintelligent traps that people in universities can fall into just because they want to seem clever or are desperate to 'belong' to the university as a machinery. The enjoyable busting of so-called 'rules of the game' is offered for building your student confidence by following useful study approaches and techniques. These are importantly based not in what is seemingly expected but in what matters intellectually – which is shown to be personal authenticity. Pat knows how to win and how to dodge dumbing down. This is through playing the game by respecting yourself and your study progress and navigating the terrain intelligently, not according to a set of instructions. The advice here is geared towards you becoming a personally effective student who can enjoy how and what you study.

Helen: So my opening question is what do you think students need to know if they are going to make the most of their university experience and enjoy themselves?

Pat: What do I think they need to already know, before they arrive, or what do they need to know to be prepared for?

Helen: 'Already know' might only possibly come about if they're reading a book like this. What do they need to come to know, what do they need to open themselves up to, in order to appreciate university, despite the negative characteristics that it has?

Pat: Yes. I would say the first thing they need to know is about themselves. How they operate. What *they* are like. If you're a haphazard learner, then you're going to have to learn to live with that way of being, as it were, in a context that wants you to be probably systematic. I think for most people learning isn't – particularly for the arts or the humanities – very systematic. You don't start by having three hours in the morning, focusing on this and then come back in the evening, focusing on that. You're kind of dipping into things. Trying things out. In some ways you have to accommodate yourself.

I'd say in a practical sense that the best way to do that is to come along with reading. With having done reading. Reading that either is going to help you find your way around or that's going to enable you to challenge yourself and your thinking. I say don't try and master things too quickly. Don't believe you have to have that business of mastery early on, because lots of the learning that's likely to go on, that will be useful to you, will be much more partial, haphazard, a bit here and bit there. Hopefully, it will link up in a way – but it takes a long, long, long time to get to a point where you are secure in your knowledge about something. Don't expect to be working your way confidently through things in an ordered and systematic way. Be prepared to try things out. To look at ideas in the context of knowing yourself and how you work.

Helen: Students, I think, are worried and become fearful of the so-called higher levels of knowledge that the university might have. They can feel inadequate in respect of the people around them, the lecturers, the others. That gets them stressed, don't you think?

Pat: I do. I think the only cure for that – maybe not a cure, but a treatment – would be to do that basic reading. Also, to take advice: if I'm doing this course, what are the two or three texts (it might be books, it might be articles) that are going to help me to get to grips with this? That I can manage to read, intelligently? University teachers often give readings out. These might be things that are not immediately, necessarily user-friendly for all students. So students have to find their own texts to guide them through. Also that question of operating at a different level suggests to me that you need to be able to make yourself solid at another level. I always used to advise education students when they were doing an education degree to read the education section of Haralambos (Haralambos and Holborn 2014), which is the A-level sociology textbook. If you can get your head around all that sociology in that textbook, which is an A-level textbook, then it will equip you really well for your degree. You will then have that foundation and anything you learn in addition to that is an advance.

Helen: So is the game how you treat knowledge? Lots of students will have been at a school. They will have been spoon-fed in so many ways. They won't actually know how knowledge operates. For instance, that some ways of coming into knowledge require a knower to be secure – to have this foundation that you're talking about – and *then* you can wander around, be a butterfly, pick and mix, all that sort of stuff. Or, the other way around. These are all strategies and techniques, aren't they and up for personal decision-making as to how to handle it? But how do students know that the path to knowledge can be creative and intuitively understood, while also involving strategy, if they've been spoon-fed up to that moment of needing a new approach appropriate for university-level research and thought? I think they might feel ill-prepared for the university study style required given how schools too often behave in handing it all over on a plate. What do you think?

Pat: An important component of that – the syndrome that you identify is to do with imagining that everyone else is more clued up than you are, that your knowledge is not yet adequate to the task. Also, that you don't know where to go next to find what you need to know. That business of understanding yourself I think is important – understanding that you're going through that. Understanding that the way round that is not to try and do too much and absorb everything but to find helpful academic or intellectual friends in the form of articles and books, that will be key inserts for you. If you look at my reading list, as an academic who has done a bit of publishing in various contexts – journals and books – my reading list is quite big but is repeated over and over. I rely on these key texts as anchors for my thinking and a student can do that with two or three texts. These don't have to be primary texts, meaning the original work of Marx or Foucault, for example. I go back to Haralambos: if you can get your head around the many important positions summarized there, although it's an A-level textbook, these can provide you with a very good basis for doing an education degree. You have to take off from there. The same principle applies, in general, to any degree and discipline. Get a foundation of knowledge.

Helen: In that sense there's no hierarchy to what knowledge is useful at any given time. You could engage with a children's book about education. It might actually inform about these positions of knowledge you are talking about. All of this – you know we could talk, you and I, for such a long time about this topic, this art of coming into knowledge: How do you do it? What are your techniques? What's your attitude? And so on. It *is* an art form, isn't it?

Pat: Getting knowledge is an art form, but I think it's very difficult. It's difficult to advise somebody in terms of offering them a programme. It's much more about helping somebody to come to terms with the acquisition of knowledge at degree level. The first thing you want to say is: don't be too demanding of yourself. The danger there is you try and you fail; big ideas get thrown at you and very often those big ideas take an awful lot of work to get hold of, to get used to, to be able to put into use. So be easy on yourself, work cannily with your sources and always do that work of translating things into your own terms even if you might be doing wrong. That means you could, for example, take Haralambos, you could take the section on Bernstein, for example – Bernstein is notoriously difficult – how long does it take to read Bernstein? He's only got five books. It's the same book five times over. But it will take you years to be able to read your way through that. But if you go to Haralambos you get a neat kind of summary of it. Maybe it doesn't do justice to all the complexities of it but you can begin then to translate that into your own terms. That's the important kind of work to do. You're always going to be borrowing and leaning on other people's ideas. That's the only way you can get knowledge or understanding. There is no other way. You can't suddenly become inventive and creative. If you do that on your own terms then that work of translation is enabling you to synthesize and interiorize ideas that are going to be of help to you.

Helen: The word 'translation' as you're using it, obviously, doesn't mean translating languages from one to the other, it means translating ideas into sense. Is that right? Is that what you mean?

Pat: Yes, translating. Another word for it is paraphrasing. Some students – and this I think is a really interesting example, at my university, we used to get students from the Middle East who would copy stuff because copying is a way of learning, but in a Western context it's not regarded as learning. It's regarded as illegitimate. It's regarded as plagiarism. But you can't actually engage with ideas unless you can copy them. So, to avoid the accusation, or danger of plagiarism, you have to do that work of *paraphrasing*. But it's also good pedagogy, good learning technique. You're having to put something into your own terms.

Some ideas – for instance, Bernstein's ideas – carry their own heavy vocabulary, which is not going to be your or my already acquired vocabulary, but it's an extension of vocabulary. The more you can make that demonstrably your own through the re-articulation of those ideas, the more successful you are likely to be. You can do that. I used to tell doctoral students that you have to read with a pencil in your hand. You're not just reading, but you're marking things and you're making notes. That kind of reading is different from reading the novel *Huckleberry Finn*. Reading with a pencil means you're not reading in a smooth flow, but you're having to interrupt your reading to go over something, make sense of it, put a ring around something, expand something, make notes as you go along.

We haven't, in my experience of the academic context, ever had the habit of teaching students how to do that kind of reading. I think that kind of reading is very important for those subject areas that trade in ideas. So, any major set of ideas. So if you wanted to get to grips with Bruno Latour, you've got an enormous body of work to grapple with, but you've got to start somewhere. You've got to start at a point where you can understand what you're doing. So you take a small segment and you say, 'this is my starting point. I'm going to get to grips with these three or four pages. I'm going to dwell on those. Thrash my way through them. Keep with them until I've got them, as it were, into my own vocabulary. So I can begin to kind of habituate those ideas, that vocabulary, to my usage.'

Helen: You're talking about the art of self-study. The art of knowledge, the art of accumulating self-knowledge, because it matters to oneself. But there are students who, possibly, are not going to university to accumulate knowledge. For reasons of cultural capital, they may not know the value of knowledge. They've ended up at university, who knows how or why, but there they are. It matters to them to be there, but they don't actually understand yet the university can offer them this profound engagement with knowledge, which is (a) what matters for success, because the university is a machinery for knowledge engagement, but (b) it is also enjoyable. Is it not? But there are students who don't appreciate any of that, and they end up at university. What can they do?

Pat: Those students must have had some experience of that, albeit limited and partial. They would also need to put it on the table in front of them, what this can be for you. Of course not everybody is in a position to take it up or to make the most of it. This is what universities, university courses don't do. They assume everybody is there because they're enamoured of whatever subject it is. The student has some vague notion of love of knowledge applied to them as a given assumption by the academic staff. As you rightly say that is not necessarily a given. It would be good for students to be *taught* that. That this experience can do this for you and it's an extension of yourself that can be quite empowering.

To learn about nineteenth-century elementary education, its formation and the pioneer bureaucrats who fed into that, it's not automatically everybody's cup of tea, as it were. *But* if you really understood that it would change the way you see the world that you live in *now*, that it would change the way you think about yourself, who you are, how you stand in relation to every university process that you're going through? There's value in training, or encouraging students at least, to see things in that way. Like I said, I think the automatic assumption is that we all know what universities are for. We all know it's a very good thing. We all know that you will benefit from it and we just kind of crack on, assuming that all our students are equally engaged in the process of becoming qualified, learning as they go along.

Helen: Do you think there's a degree of chance in all of this stumbling onto the beauty of knowledge thing? I remember when I was an undergraduate, I was dis-enamoured by the philosophy course because it was analytic. I'm not really an analytic philosopher by nature. So, I sort of disengaged from the course. I thought this isn't for me, oh dear, I've made a mistake choosing this course. It wasn't what I expected. But then one day I was just sitting down in my room and I thought, I think I'd better read a book. So I picked up Kierkegaard, *Fear and Trembling* (Kierkegaard 1985) – I have no idea why – and *it blew my mind*. At university there was one book that I read, but I *really* read it. It was that Jacques Derrida thing where in that film he says, 'I haven't read all the books here on these library shelves, but the ones that I've read, I really have read very well.'

So at university as an undergraduate, I can say I read one book and I really mean that. It's true. But what the reading of that one book did for me was it opened up the idea that you can have your mind blown by forms of knowledge. I never forgot that. It started my education proper, that one book, which has never ceased as a road of self-study. I was so impressed by what that book did to my mind, I wanted the effect again and again. But I'd got lucky just once! I didn't know at all at that time *how* to search for good reading and pursue a line of enquiry. The university did nothing to help me learn what that might mean. A reading list or lecture does not do that entrance-into-self-through-knowledge thing, nor help you understand why being motivated to look for knowledge will matter to you personally if you stick at it, sifting through some weaker materials to get to the good literature and work. Despite being a university student, an intelligent, literate person, who could hold a conversation of sorts and engage with books superficially, I had no clue how to read. In fact I'd say university was getting in the way of my reading. The university had not succeeded in reaching me and telling me I was worth knowledge. I suspect it fails millions of people that way every year. Which is why this book we're engaged with here, in this conversation, matters. We have to do the work here, for students, that universities neglect to engage with: the bridge across to *owning* knowledge for oneself.

Pat: There are a number of things I would say. First of all, the idea of the beauty, the love of knowledge. I think it's just romantic nonsense, really. Knowledge is only loveable if it enhances you in some way, your sense of yourself. In some way it has to materially add to, not just your pleasure, but your pleasure in yourself as a competent being. Students are expected to already arrive with that idea somehow, already be in a position of feeling competent. If you were in my class and I was teaching analytic philosophy, which I will be quite happy to teach about, I'd say you're not either an analytic or not an analytic philosopher, it's just that analytic philosophy simply hasn't spoken to you. I had a smart, astute colleague who once said to me when we were discussing something, 'Oh, I don't talk about Bernstein.' She had chosen not to go there. She was a very sophisticated person and could have made the effort to go there, but she'd decided not to. The idea is not that analytic philosophy isn't for you, that you're innately un-attuned to it, it's that you never found a way into it. It hasn't spoken to you. The trick is to make it find a way for *it* to speak to *you*. That's the thing I think a lot of students struggle with. Nineteenth-century formation of state-sponsored education doesn't speak to students automatically. Of course it doesn't! So you have to find a way of making it so it can enhance your understanding of the things you want to understand.

Helen: I think it's possible based on my own postgraduate experience – interacting with different forms of knowledge or different disciplines – for a person to find their way into any discipline. There's never a hopeless situation.

Pat: I agree entirely with that. We are encouraged to think of ourselves as relating to knowledge as segmented, that it is in institutionally separated categories, types and taxonomies. That is probably a product of curricularization. Thereby we can decide, 'I can't do math, that's not for me.' I worked with people who are historians, and they used to say, 'I'm a historian, I can't do that theory stuff.' I used to think 'well, if you can't do theory, you can't really be a historian, can you . . .'. From their perspective it was a way of saying, 'Look, leave off. I can't, I haven't got the energy, the time, the dedication, the devotion to get into *that* because I'm in *this* space and I have accommodated myself to this. I'm happy to work here.' For students who are having to expose themselves to new knowledge, they don't have the luxury to say, 'No, I'm not doing that.' They need to have some kind of way of understanding the process that will enable them to access knowledge, which in many cases it's a series of ideas wrapped up in a specific vocabulary. That kind of training, like I said, I don't think it happens very much. They'll teach you all sorts of stuff about how to do a dissertation. They'll give you a formula for doing it. A wrong one, actually. But they won't teach you how to accommodate yourself to new ideas, perspectives, ways of understanding forms of knowledge.

Most students who are successful have to do that for themselves. Most of them do it because they have a strong interest, a strong investment. They are highly motivated and they will grapple with it and do it. But again, you know, you could train people how to do that. You could do it at a very basic level. I used to get postgraduate students, for example – in order to build up their awareness and understanding of the topic area they were engaging with for their doctoral thesis – I used to get them to collect abstracts. Then they could identify what were the given positions, what were the key orientations and the most important for them. An abstract will always tell you what its theoretical perspective is. That's a shorthand for doing a lot of reading, one that will practically help you to engage with ideas.

Helen: That sense of shortcuts to an engagement with ideas is one seasoned academics have grasped a hold of as the way to survive, but also an entirely legitimate way to engage with knowledge. I remember my surprise and shock – initial horror even – when a university career professor-mentor in my first job said you didn't need to read the whole of the article; that you could read the abstract and then skim through sometimes – but it's true. Students seem to me to be so fearful of taking shortcuts. They have a sense that they have to read the whole book, or they've got to read at least ten articles in full and only then, maybe, they'll start to know something. They need to hear there are legitimate ways to do things such as this. You can be rough and dirty with it, when you're wading through a vast sea of literature or searching for a path forwards, an argument to make, a thesis to consider. At the start, certainly.

Pat: Yes. Nobody has read Bernstein purely by reading Bernstein. Anybody who has ever read Bernstein has also had to rely on summary, on the cheats, the hack versions, the simplifications, some of the paraphrasers and so on – because that's your way in. Then you can go back and if you want to, read the hard-core Bernstein material. But you can't do that really just by starting with Bernstein and sticking with Bernstein, ploughing your way through it. It's pretty much impossible to do that, without assistance from some kind of translator facility sitting beside you. That's the metaphor I would use.

Helen: The art of getting to Bernstein, in your example here, is to read a whole host of easy guides to Bernstein. To the point where when you read Bernstein you already have some expertise in Bernstein, and then Bernstein himself tells you the real thing with his own voice.

Pat: You might not be an expert, but you're familiar with the concepts. You have some emerging understanding of the meaning of the word 'code'. Some kind of grasp of what code theory might be. The kinds of things that theory deals with, the area and the implications as well as for education. Social class in relation to education. That's a big thing if you can get those rudimentary things securely under your belt, confidently, and be able to make reference to Bernstein. It's a big thing. You know, it really is.

Helen: I remember you mentioning someone and saying, 'I don't think he's ever read Derrida', but he kept citing Derrida. You weren't being complementary of that person's scholarship. There was the suggestion that they were getting things wrongs with their claims and the way they were citing. So there's a limit to how rough and dirty you can be. If you're going to cite Derrida or Bernstein you actually have to have an informed confidence that you're doing it in the right way. Otherwise, you're going to make a hash of it.

Pat: I'm not advocating that it's a substitute but, you know, Derrida has about sixty published books now and he keeps publishing them, even though he died years ago! How does he do that?! Nobody, nobody, *nobody* has *really* read all those books. So nobody is in a position to be able to speak authoritatively about the whole thing. But what you can do is you can say I'm going to read around and then focus on these two or three pages in this book by Derrida as his original voice, not paraphrased. I'll use those as my point of entry into this bigger frame of ideas and these are legitimate academic practices, ways into fields of knowledge. Derrida is notoriously difficult. Sure. Anything which is not already familiar to you is difficult. When you go to university, for whatever reason or in whatever identity, you opt, in a sense, for a life that is partially but significantly academic. That's inevitably part of wrestling with new ways of seeing things, understanding, writing, speaking, new vocabularies. That's a really important part of it, as well as technical competences. We're only here talking about that one aspect to the academic life, which I think is interesting: that it takes up so much time to consider and to know how to practice the getting of knowledge.

Helen: This technology of entering into confidence with knowledge is important for students, isn't it? Otherwise they're going to get really stressed. I'll give you a metaphor, an example if you like of here, this garden. This is a new garden for me since I moved to Italy. It's big. There are all kinds of things about the level of countryside that this garden presents to me with that last year really freaked me out. An immediate recent example I can think of, because it was only yesterday, is that I realized I'm no longer stressed by dealing with the storage of wood. Last year, as a countryside beginner, I didn't know that if you put wood directly on the soft earth without creating supports underneath your woodpile to allow air to circulate a bit, the bottom layer of wood in contact with the earth is going to become mouldy. Yesterday when I started to stack a pile of wood I knew it. I don't know how I picked this up. I just worked it out. I put these air supports down on the ground first and then I started to stack up my pile. It felt great because I felt in charge. I felt capable, I felt like I knew wood stacking. I used to feel the same about academic work when I was a beginner student: freaked out by my inexperience. Slowly I picked up how to write, how to manage references, how to find literature, how to read with shortcuts and then in full when required or desired, how to construct an argument, how to signpost sections in an argument. Stick by stick, with the right base you could say. The air circulated after a while, but at first my academic practice was inevitably causing mould while I learned how to do it, sitting right on the rain-clogged ground. It's the same for students with their knowledge acquisition. It's a journey.

Pat: Yes, the student journey is about learning the techniques for the technology of learning. It isn't really taught to students. Just like you clearly didn't have local advice to hand about stacking wood. You were on your own. Students are on their own. It would be better if they weren't, because their stakes are higher than a few lost branches.

Helen: Quite. There are very different techniques to learn at university than at school. There children and young people copy and parrot, through forms of performance. While university remains about performance, the techniques to learn require independence and originality. It's more of a creative way?

Pat: Well, it's supposed to be more independent.

Helen: It has to be because the lecturers don't want to know you outside their office hours.

Pat: That's right. So you are automatically, immediately expected to be an independent learner. You are expected to arrive as an independent mind.

Helen: But isn't that stressful? If you arrive and you're expected to be an independent learner and you've never learned independently? Is that why so many students are stressed out so badly?

Pat: Yes, but also I think it means that for many university life is a disappointment. In the academic sense at least, because they don't have that kind of close guiding relationship with the teacher. They're not in a position to take what the university experience has to offer, which is around that kind of independent learning, being able to guide your own reading and understanding of things to a significant degree, even when you're on a curriculum.

Helen: The first few days of undergraduate life at university for me, they did a tour for students of the library, which I missed. But had I turned up to it, they would have said, 'Here is the library desk, here is the section on this, here are the articles, this is how you check out a book and so on.' I went to one as a postgraduate – the format isn't maybe vastly different across award levels. They would have given me knowledge and guidance of all of the library facilities. University librarians always strike me as very thorough and professional. But at no point would they have said to me, those librarians, 'And you need to *come to* the library, *by the way!*' That bit is what we are talking about. The library doesn't function at all for you unless you go to it.

Pat: Yes. You need to find your way around books, journal articles, and learn how to read them, make use of them, dip into them in some cases. So all that business of being a crafty learner – that's never taught. In my experience, I don't think I've ever seen it being taught.

Helen: Do they even teach that you have to turn up? That you have to turn up to lectures, that you have to turn up to the library door and walk through it. As an undergraduate I could have done with that message.

Pat: Nah, they don't say that. They assume you know that. Although, if you don't turn up to lectures now there's usually some 'feedback' after three or four occasions. But the expectation is that because you're an independent learner, you will take responsibility for your own attendance and learning. Back in the day, before things became more instrumentalized, it was very free and easy. It was always assumed you were making intelligent choices about what you wanted and where you wanted to be. Or at least making choices. Whether they were intelligent or not is perhaps another question.

Helen: Well, that would have been valid as an experience twenty-five years ago when I was an undergraduate. Nobody said a word to me. One lecturer once said, 'you're not really turning up very much.' Three years, just one person said, 'where are you?' I attended something like 20 per cent of the course, if that, but no one cared, least of all me. I just didn't know doing the course could have mattered to me and could have been awesome. No one said anything about that: the inside of the offer. I think they should have. I had a college tutor. I was surrounded by other students. Why was it not a matter for discussion in the air? How to play the university game! Some people found the game, I could tell. They were really into it but somehow I felt on the outside of it all, not excluded, but un-included. I'm sure other students today feel like that and battle to own it, take their role up in the game and try to win. I think they might have felt like I did, which is as a non-player.

Pat: I remember when I was a postgraduate, I went to the first session and I didn't go to anymore. I got a distinction in that paper but I did it on my own. That was OK because *the assumption* is you're doing it on your own.

Helen: As a postgraduate I think it's easier to combine not turning up with performing well. As an undergraduate, fresh out of school, if you don't turn up you are more likely to get lost and lose out. If you take that experience of undergrad where I turned up to nothing, and then you take the experience of postgrad where I turned up to everything, sometimes two or three times, I did those things over and over again. The difference is the first time I didn't know that I was *free* to turn up. Isn't that crazy! I mean, I didn't turn up because there was just not that technology of learning and there was not the self-motivation. There was not the ownership in any way of learning or knowledge, apart from, as I said, that one book I read. Whereas by the time I was a postgrad fifteen years later, that knowledge was *mine*. It belonged to Helen and no one else. Mine to take. Mine to get. Mine to use. I wanted it and it mattered to me. For that reason, I turned up two or three times to things. Not to miss any detail of something that was mine to have. Students struggle, it seems to me, to own knowledge. Have they got low self-esteem when it comes to having knowledge of their own? I think they deserve to *own* knowledge. I wish they would. The world rather needs people who own their minds and the expanding of their minds these days, more than ever. It's frustrating to see people not take it. Elites do. They take it all. They know how to take. If all students, from every background, would *take* the knowledge, own it, I think they would equalize things up. But that happens too rarely. What's going on?

Pat: I would say they've been trained to think like that.

Helen: What do you mean?

Pat: Education as we know it is the training in understanding that kind of knowledge hierarchy. You're a student and that means you are positioned in such a way that you are subordinated to the system of knowledge and to those who are invested in it and qualified.

Helen: Ouch. By postgraduate level I wasn't subordinated, but age eighteen, as an undergraduate, I clearly was. Undergraduate students *should not* be subordinate to a knowledge hierarchy. I would say no student, of *any* educational level, should be. But at university it's even more vital they feel intellectually free and powerful. Especially if they want to play the university at its own game: the supposed freedom to think new thoughts.

Pat: It's a function of schooling that we have that kind of attitude towards knowledge as something which belongs to a curriculum, an institution, to those qualified into the institution. That hierarchical division between learners and teachers is very, very significant. It continues through to the university and is there in so many features. Perhaps most dramatically at postgraduate level where the supervisor relationship is very restricting. The academy has set up a model of a thesis. This was being purveyed as the nature of things. There's no specification in any academic context of what a doctoral thesis should contain, what form it should take. Yet this very specific format was being purveyed and had become accepted almost universally as the norm.

I have had colleagues becoming absolutely livid at the fact that I was encouraging students to avoid doing a literature review. I was calling it an idiotic concept for these reasons, you don't want to do that because you may want to take your thinking in some other kind of direction, representing some other mode, because it doesn't match up with the basic knowledge and research relations. But this was like a violation of everything that these professionally very powerful people had come to understand as the nature of things, the way to do things. That kind of formalized thinking – it's really an ontological enclosure – had infected almost every kind of dimension, such that there was very little room for thinking or being otherwise. That translates also into what kinds of ideas were acceptable.

Education is particularly prone to that kind of limitation, that restriction. It was very controversial one year because I had an undergraduate who had written his dissertation in the form of an exchange of letters. But that wasn't the formula. Where was the literature review? Where was the research method? It didn't look like what was considered to be a dissertation. So I think academic life is very highly regulated, very closely protected from intrusions. I think that students are trained from very early on to see themselves as the subordinate partners in that learning process. You learn in relation to what the curriculum says you have to learn and in relation to the teacher who is very often doing their best to give you what the curriculum specifies. That training is a training in subordination. At what stage do you claim the right to become an independent learner capable of claiming the right to not just shape the knowledge that you have, but to declare what it is and what it is doing? I don't think anybody ever securely gets to that point because you're always under that peer review pressure at a later stage. You mustn't violate the principles of genre. Genre is fairly sacrosanct. Even the most apparently revolutionary thinkers – Derrida is a really good example – he's completely refreshing in some dimensions of his thinking, but he's completely slavish in other ways in his obeisance to the idea of literature. That's a very common thing. Foucault is meticulously scholarly. His extremely original ideas can only be represented because they are painstakingly worked out. His references are ordered, frequent, exhaustive. Even he has to play that game.

Helen: It's a game.

Pat: But it's a game of high stakes. Just because it's a game doesn't mean it's trivial. It's not trivial pursuits – ☺

Helen: I don't think students realize that we are playing a game that is high stakes and that sometimes we are playing it for their sake. For instance, a student might do a dissertation made up of letters and you, the lecturer, might read it and think what a brilliant piece of work. Fantastic! But the second marker says, 'I can't believe you've given it a first, this is not even a pass!' Then the academics end up in a fight for the student's sake and who's going to win? It's not a guarantee that the one that gave it the first because it's a brilliant piece of work will win. They might actually have to retract and then every year is affected, their relationships with colleagues are affected. This is war. Not just a game.

Pat: I certainly recognize that description very well. Yes, it's very risky. How to negotiate that? How to play that game? I think students should be trained in understanding of that aspect of the context. I remember this guy who got a leadership position at the university. He was just so thrilled with himself because he'd got to this position. He came to the department to give a talk about the nature of his work and what research was. He'd just sold himself entirely to this idea that he was doing important work and it was helping the world to become a better place. He'd slotted exactly into – and that is why he'd become very successful, institutionally very powerful – the order of things. But to go against the grain of that carries risks. You're right. Students would be advised to understand those risks. Some understanding of the kind of world that you're entering into. But that implies distance from the dominant ethic of the university. The dominant idea is that you're here to improve yourself, so long as you abide by the rules and regulations and demonstrate thereby that you are proper and fit to be a student.

Helen: But that's the violence.

Pat: Yes. But like you say, you can resist that violence. But at a cost. Be aware of what you are going into. What the stakes are and what you can get from it. What you have to balance against the terms of their freedoms and submissions, I would say. I think you can do that in a book: you can offer insight into that world. You don't have to say, 'this is a terrible place where violence will be done unto you.' You can say, 'One way of looking at it is in these terms and you need to be aware that there are these forces at play.' You can engage with this in this way, or that way. You can be compliant and you can take risks here and there where you see an opportunity to do that and then play safely here and there. But you do have to negotiate that dimension of risk in that world.

Helen: I think that is what the title has become.

Pat: You mean the reference to the game?

Helen: Yes. *Playing* that university game. It's in the context of what we're talking about and also what the other conversations have been talking about. The violence of the game, the joy of playing it because it's complicated and risky. It's a beautiful game in a way, but you don't want to die on account of playing.

Pat: Sure. I agree. It's good to think about the implications of that. It's a bit like football. The rules are there. The pitch is laid out in a certain way, and the time frame is given, but there's *a lot going on in the game* that's not there in the rules nor in the tactics.

Helen: I didn't know that!

Pat: You can elbow somebody. You can say something disgusting into their ear. You can trip them up, when the referee's not looking. You can play in a certain kind of way. You can target a vulnerable player. All sorts of things you can do *as part of the game*. That's why people make reference to gamesmanship, don't they. There is playing the game in ways which are outside formal, explicit parameters, as another dimension.

Helen: I suppose there's one last question then, if you could tell us what the gamesmanship of being a university student is, in a nutshell?

Pat: I think it does vary because some people are more into it than others, but certainly from my point of view it was always that wrestling with your familiarity with some ideas and your absolute unfamiliarity with others. Your desire to go beyond yourself. How do you negotiate that? I did English as an undergraduate and I'd read Lawrence, Dostoevsky, Tolstoy but I hadn't read Jane Austen or George Eliot, and so how did I manage that? Those gaps. I had to come to some kind of understanding of those things: How do I work that in? How do I negotiate that with myself? Also, how do I manage my own targets? My university experience was also a matter of managing what else was going on in my life at that time. It's not just about reading.

4

Writing Is the Way to Win

*T*his conversation with Alya, who has specialist, in-depth knowledge of the full spectrum of experiences involved in student academic work, talks about the processes involved in studying at university. The dialogue outlines the various important stages, approaches and attitudes that you as a student – each of you having, of course, your own unique background and needs – can use to create the best possible outcomes in your studies. Alya also mentions some key preconditions for doing well. The conversation considers student emotional life in the university in respect of applying oneself to studying. The optimal student grade is discussed, but to play and win the game is seen as part of a holistic student world view. Understanding what it means to be a successful student is discussed as responsible care of the functional and practical details of university life. We talk about this as a part of the bigger picture of personally achieving and ensuring a good time at university.

Helen: What do you think students need if they're going to win this university game?

Alya: There is an issue with that. Which is the very concept of winning anything. Normally winning is some kind of show in a competition. That's the basic concept of winning. Students, when they study at any given university, are not in a competition as such. Nobody is actually fighting them to get to that place. If they are good enough, they are going to reach the end. I don't think it is winning in that sense. Perhaps the word you are using as I understand it is 'succeeding'. Because at university nobody is against them. Certainly not in the culture that we teach in the West. The more we look towards Central Europe and Eastern Europe, then, it's a completely different matter. There, often teachers actually can be against you. It's a culture of catching you out and finding out what you *can't* do, whereas the culture here in Britain is to find out what people *can* do. There is no value in finding out what someone can't do in exam conditions.

I think at university, in order to succeed, because this was your original question, a student needs to understand some fundamental things. First of all, that they are doing it for themselves. This is the motivation behind the entire academic process. Some students do not go to university because they want to go to university. They go because they are pushed. Some students are pushed by family mainly and sometimes other factors. Such as 'oh, it's the best thing I can do out of all the things out there'. This is a problematic sort of motivation for people, if that is their 'willingness' to do something. They need to understand that they do it for themselves actually because they're going to be the sole beneficiary of the university education. The right kind of motivation is essential.

The other issue is understanding what it takes to do well. It takes a number of things. I'm not going to go through all of them because I'm not a specialist in them all, but writing for examination[1] – which is when writing actually matters in university study – is pretty much among the top requirements. Writing for examination is the only way that a university has – well, I think it counts for between 80 per cent and 85 per cent – for it to actually assess the quality in the work of the students, in order to give them a grade. It is the only medium we have to see what the student has learned and what they can do with what they have learned.

Students believe that if their knowledge of their subject is good enough then they are going to get a good mark. Because that's what matters. Sure, you need to know your subject. In fact, that is not sufficient. *You need to write it well.* If you write it well, your examiner will be able to appreciate that you are good at your subject. But if you don't write it well, then your examiner is *not* going to appreciate that you are good in your subject. There is no difference between what we think and what we say and *actually* what we write. This is one of the fundamental misconceptions that students have. Not just students but faculty as well. Where they believe that somehow what they mean – that is the semantics – is better than their skill of writing academically and therefore should matter more. It can't matter more because access to that semantics – which is implied in their own heads – is not available to anyone unless it is written well on paper. Writing it down is the only medium we have. It is like trying to get to university very fast but without taking the bus. The bus being the only medium – in this analogy – to actually get to university on time for your lecture. It doesn't matter how much you do want to get to university on time and how prepared you are to leave the house with your bag and everything else, unless you get onto the medium of transportation you're not going to get to university on time. This is the theory of the medium. Our sole means. Which is why students must appreciate that it is, most often, the only thing that would make a difference between a grade level. I've talked to so many students and I get the question, 'What can I do to get to the next level? How do I do it?' For example they say, 'I have a 2:2 level currently, I need a 2:1. How do I do that?' I will give them this answer, 'Your writing needs to be improved so that your knowledge looks a lot better than it is looking at the moment.' Writing is the tool people need: to convince their examiners that they know their subject, and they can actually handle that subject. Once the examiners know this then they are going to give them a better mark, possibly.

Helen: How do the students who have English as a second language cope with that when the university expects writing in English?

Alya: Well, most of them don't cope with that. So the issue that we actually have with second-language students is that they believe their problem is writing because their results are poor and they get that comment all the time. Their problem is not writing. They come to a course of academic writing and it's the wrong course for them to attend. Their problem is English. These are two different things. They are fundamentally two different things. The level of language acquisition, the linguistic ability is a different matter to writing academically. In fact, people who write academically well are only the people who can speak the language very well. And I have seen no evidence to the contrary. I do use myself as an example for this, because English is my second language. You can't hope to write academically unless you speak the language properly. What happens on paper is an exercise of moving grammatical construction and semantics from your head onto the paper. Therefore they need to exist in your head correctly. I can hear the thought before it has a graphical expression on paper. I have to say time and time again to the students, it's not academic writing education you need, you need English education. The courses that I teach are for people who are already good with speaking English. My courses do not help people who struggle with English as a language itself. So yes, there is a struggle there, but part of the struggle comes from a misunderstanding. That people who have English as a second language believe that they need writing education. But they don't need writing education. That is the second stage. The first stage is they need English language tuition. And that is a completely different discipline.

Helen: That makes a lot of sense. I remember teaching academic writing with full lecture theatres and a lot, most, of the people there had English as a second language. They were hoping that that course would sort their problems out.

Alya: We see that every time. It's pretty much the status quo when it comes to the question that you asked. That's how it is. That's why universities have departments specialized in handling this issue for international students. That's where the students need to go. For pre-sessional courses. This is where students go before they start their first year. And these are courses supposed to handle English language difficulties that they have before they actually come into the English speaking culture.

Helen: But isn't the demand to write well academically a very large or high one? Because if I think about my own academic writing – I'm an English mother tongue speaker and all my childhood and then adult life I've been, what I thought was, a writer. I was doing the PhD and subsequently moving into an academic career – that is a stage of maturity in respect of age that is more than that which most undergraduates have, so maybe I was at an advantage in that respect – but I found, I *assumed* that I could write and so I therefore wrote. Then what I discovered, it came as a huge shock, was that there are certain genres of writing in academia. You have to *learn* them. You have to *practice* them. You can't assume that you're a good writer. That is something that comes out of, as you say, a very high level of English awareness, plus of course all the knowledge, the research, the reading. And when you're putting it together, it's a really complicated game at the start, certainly to get it right. Well, I had the English no problem. But to write? It was and is a constant journey. Some people are more talented or more adept, better suited to it, than others. I rewrote so many things so many times, obviously quickly in my case, because I speak English fluently and without doubt, but I rewrote so many times. I mean, how do these students get to a place where they can write academically if I find it really complicated as a game of presentation? I have had years of practice now so the level of challenge has diminished, but students don't get those long years of apprenticeship. I might be assuming things about myself there, but if *I* find it hard, with my background and development curve, how on earth are students expected to do it well in a short space of time?

Alya: Well. I think the expectation from departments is not necessarily expressed in those terms. I think the university expects everybody to write at the level required for them to be examined. In other words, as a bare minimum. That really is the very bottom of quality. Departments need to be able to read texts which *make sense* in English. An idea can be read by an examiner and understood so they can give it a mark. That level of writing, I call it the very rock bottom because it can be grammatically mistaken and it often is. In other words, you can form communication which still maintains grammatical errors and it will somehow still make sense. It will make sense at the very, very basic level. It would not make sense at a level that would enable an examiner to appreciate the mental sophistication of formulating that bit of knowledge so that they can give them a *better* mark. It will not do that. Also a text that is submitted with grammatical errors will also be downgraded because that is on any marking criteria sheet that examiners might use: to take marks away for writing poor English. So this is what the university would expect. They would expect people to write well enough for an examiner to be able to make sense of what they have said. There is no standard actually given, apart from the fact that you must write correctly. Your text needs to be grammatically correct. That is an actual expectation. And you need to display your level of knowledge as compatible with you passing this test or passing this exam, or having the minimum grade in order to declare a pass. But I have not seen an actual written standard, at the level of instruction, for what academic writing should look like. Because that in itself, even if somebody was asked to formulate such a standard, if I was asked, it would be very, very hard to actually do so. The process has so many factors. Therefore universities have to be satisfied asking students to submit texts that they can actually read and understand, so that they can give the submissions a mark.

Helen: In respect of the stress that I've noticed quite a few students in lots of different places encounter? Also which I encountered as a student. I can't think of anybody I've ever spoken to, who has been open – some people don't talk about it, of course – who hasn't said it was stressful in some way to be a university student. And this being that the act of writing in a university environment seems to the uninitiated as some kind of mystery, a mystery of excellence. It seemingly strikes fear into their hearts until they realize, as I did, that actually it's not mysterious at all. There are ways to do it. There is a mechanism of doing it. Which I would identify as: you need to read a lot and you need to think a lot. Then you need to – and you're speaking about this part – put those thoughts down on paper in a convincing way, a clear way. That means clear in lots of senses: structure, grammar, signposting between sections so they follow each other coherently, so it's readable. Hopefully, it might reach the next level, beyond mere clarity. This would be that it's stimulating for the reader, in a university environment anyway. All this is a package which I find now quite mechanical, but students new to a university writing demand find it frightening. They haven't had this practice and they haven't gone through the cycle of worrying about it, getting it done, submitting it and then finding out that actually it worked out fine and they got a mark that they were reasonably happy with or not – whatever the outcome was. Once they've been through a few of those cycles, maybe by the third year or something, the mystery will have disappeared. They'll just get on with it as a form of work. Do you have an opinion about this mystery side of things? How students can deal with the stress of the unknown when it comes to academic writing?

Alya: Well, I think it has a lot to do with realizing what is at play. What the difficulties are. Knowledge is power. That is true in this sense as well. So once you know what the issue is, then you have a level of empowerment to deal with that. Even if that level of empowerment is the knowledge 'oh I need to ask for help about this, because this is an actual issue'. So the truly helpless out there are the people who do not know they, in fact, need the help, until it strikes them very, very hard when they receive their writing back.

One of the first things that I recommend to students is that they work on the knowledge of what the difficulties are. They will get to this if they allow for their work to be examined at least once and returned to them. The first approach in dealing with what your difficulties are and the resulting stress is the feedback that comes from examiners. Some people take feedback seriously. Some people dismiss it as criticism. I don't want to discuss that here, because that is the emotional impact and to give in to that is certainly not the right way to move forwards productively. Feedback contains what it should contain: what students need to know – to understand what needs to be addressed. Then with these insights there are a range of things that we can do to address difficulties.

The other tool in handling stress, once you've understood what the issues are, is to understand that improvement will not happen overnight. It is an incremental process. That means step by step. A length of time. Now the length of time when it comes to university life happens best if it is done in a structured way, at the level of a timetable. This is where a lot of students fail, because without a timetable and not knowing how to spend their time, time trickles away. We get into the complaint level of 'oh, I never have time to actually submit', when in fact students really do have a lot of time to submit. What I'm trying to say is that once difficulties are identified from feedback, then the student can address stress if they devise for themselves a plan, a plan set against time. One of the greatest triggers of anxiety and stress is when people understand they are out of time. A timetable, on a daily basis to handle difficulties with writing, helps you to see achievement. If at the end of that day's timetable you have not actually done what you're supposed to do, that is an underachievement. In other words, if the immediate perception is now I'm out of time because I didn't succeed in doing what I planned to achieve, that would increase stress. Underachievement increases stress, (over)achievement reduces stress. In reducing stress self-esteem increases because self-esteem is not a given, it's a variable. General well-being does rely a lot on self-esteem as well, not just levels of stress.

So, if students are able to identify (1) what the difficulties are and (2) what they need to do to handle these difficulties and set them along a timetabled plan, then they will have a realistic chance for their stress to go down. But there is waiting in this process. The waiting I'm referring to is for things to actually get better, with the right steps. A lot of students will not understand that things have gotten better until they submit for the next exam. So they need to wait for the second round of feedback. This allows them to see whether they have actually gotten better. If they have or when they have, that stress level would go down. All of this is a process. So the short answer to your question about how they deal with stress is to actually understand it is a process that needs to be devised by themselves. It's architecture, just like academic writing – the process is architectural. You need to find the pieces in order to build the wonderful building that will serve as your shelter, so to speak.

Helen: It strikes me this is difficult. You make it sound easy but it's a puzzle to fit together, no? The time, the devising of the process, the timetable and the waiting that students are required to do themselves, to answer the issues that arise by identifying what they need to strengthen, in order to win at university. A lot of students who go to university have been to schools. Schools have fed them everything they needed in order to jump through hoops. That's a fact. So when they come to you, to university, it's a different atmosphere, wouldn't you say? A freer atmosphere and that freedom is a challenge.

Alya: Yes. Absolutely. For them there is no transition or for many of them, depending what educational culture they come from. In most cases there is no transition as such. The university does try to create some sort of induction. These days you have even pre-induction programmes, in order to provide some sort of transition from school to university. But it really doesn't work. Not in reality. When they come to university, there is a state of the tree branch you were standing on, that they had been used to standing on, suddenly being cut off. There is a weightlessness about it, and that is a very anxious thing.

What contributes to that as well is being away from home. People who are actually at home for university do better. Most people are not at home. In fact, a lot of people are countries away from home. Some of them are one ocean away from where they grew up and their families and established friends. So for them it is very, very hard. That transition doesn't come with instructions. A school system can't mimic a university system. It's not possible. Anywhere. Whereas the university system has no need to maintain a school system. That's why the students have chosen to go to the university: to go to the next level. As in any game to borrow your terminology – that you play on a screen – the next level no longer cares about the level before. It's completely done and dusted. This is how gaming becomes addictive by the way, because you must attain the next level all the time. The next level will bring a reward. So it's a psychological trick. But anyway, that's a different discussion.

Helen: Although relevant to issues around belief in needing higher education attendance.

Alya: There is an incompatibility in philosophy between a school system and a university system. A school system cannot afford, doesn't know how, does not have the resources and the age of learners, for it to mimic the university system of higher education. Students are not mature enough at school level to deal with university-style demands, whereas the university no longer has the need or any interest whatsoever to maintain a previous level. That would be detrimental to itself in its quest to provide the next level of education.

Helen: That transition to self-study and self-management – what you call the devising of a process that allows students to succeed and incrementally so – is a very difficult one if psychologically you are expecting to be told what to do and how to do it, and you've never encountered self-determination.

Alya: Absolutely. That is absolutely true. Which is why we need to also pay attention to the fact that the different award levels at university actually handle this issue. At undergraduate level there is still a lot of spoon feeding. The students are given a timetable. That's to start with. That is a huge help. The timetable is the only institutional device that they know from school. But once a timetable is provided, the students immediately make the assumption that this is what it is going to be like for me now. They take it to be the absolute truth, a timetable. Right, so this is still a lot of spoon feeding and that spoon feeding also goes into master's level. Taught masters also have a timetable. So still the university is telling them a *lot* of what they have to do. Only when it gets to research level such as masters by research and PhD does this change fundamentally. There is very little given to you, to the point that there is no timetable and you need to captain the ship *completely* in every single aspect of that encounter.

I think the difficulty is that the students, when given a timetable as an example of the university telling them what to do, take it to mean that we can act exactly as we used to at school. They don't know any different. But it doesn't work for them to think like that. At university level there is a lot of other work, which is way above and beyond the timetable.

At university there is also the life aspect. Students are no longer at home. The life aspects mean they now need to live for themselves. That is not a timetable. Cooking is not a timetable. The going to a shop to buy what you need to eat and to do the thinking about what you need to buy, questions to pose to oneself such as 'What do I need in order to survive tomorrow, or have something to eat tomorrow, or be entertained?' It's no longer done for you at university. The world does not function as it used to function at school. I would imagine that is a pretty hard hit for students – especially first years.

Helen: It's asking a lot.

Alya: Yes.

Helen: This book is saying, ultimately, that the way to win is to write well. Then alongside this there has to be, for the sake of these students, acknowledgement – out of empathy and compassion and understanding of the predicament and the situation of all of this traumatic transition – of their heavy new burdens. The potentially traumatic transition. You know, it's not enough for the book to say 'you write, you win!' That's not how it works. Or 'you write, you succeed'. While it is true, it's, as you are pointing to, much more complicated. It's much deeper than that. That one can get to writing at all, among everything going on, well it's definitely to start to win.

Alya: Yes. That's a good summary. So in order to get to writing well you need to be able to do a lot of other things that perhaps nobody has ever taught you. Speaking of which, I suppose the background you come from actually plays a role. People have different levels of exposure to life's roughness, belonging to, depending on, where they come from, what sort of lifestyles they have had. Which is why you would see that students coming from certain countries would do better under stress and demand than students coming from the UK. The level of life demand for them had been very different to the level of life demand of students brought up in the UK. So that also plays a role. And this is something that the university literally can't help you with. We don't have a system to handle preconditions. There's no way. There are so many of these educational and social preconditions that students come with, which are not part of the university business. In an ideal world – this is utopic – there would be an institution between the school and university. It would function as an equalizing device. No matter what background you come from, country, life experience, you are given the opportunity before you come to get to the same level, before you actually enter university.

Helen: The literature...

Alya: I'm trying to tell you there is no equality. But I'm not sure you want to put that in your book. There certainly isn't.

Helen: I suppose in a way the ambition of the book is to equalize. To level things up. By giving those students who don't have the background, as you put it, the cultural capital to understand the need to deal with preconditions in a sane, rational, careful, planned and processed way, to give them a head start. A heads up that they are about to enter into a very complicated situation and these are the factors and the features of that situation. So they can prepare or take affirmative action in their best interests. Things that the book certainly can't do for them. It's asking them to realize they need to do it for themselves.

My sense of the university is that it is good at having a great library. It is good at enjoying writing and reading and debating and studying and researching. Sometimes good at teaching. All of these kinds of things. It's there for those reasons. It's not there to be a mummy or daddy, or a carer. Yet lots of people who enter into universities need those things, good versions of care, much more than they need to read and write or get a certificate. If no one is around to do that care for them then they need to get busy on it themselves. A lot of the benefit and the joy of the university is being wasted while these students are dealing with the other stuff, when they could be accessing the brilliance and the benefit of the university. It strikes me as a terrible waste of what a university is good at and good for, that very few people are sorted in the self-care aspects required, such that they can easily access the library with joy, for example, or experience undiluted joy at picking up a book. Not having their mind wandering off into other things that are causing them stress. Just because they haven't quite got their process sorted. I know at that age or in those circumstances it is complicated. Naturally. But you only get a certain window to get into that library with an institutional library card and to read a book and then have access to the professors who can discuss it with you or to discuss it with fellow students studying similar material.

Access to a university experience of joy – the fast route to it – seems to be to focus on getting the writing sorted. Doing everything you possibly can for that. Which sort of takes care of the other stuff along the way. For example, if you're planning to write well, you need to take care of all these things you've identified or else you can't get to the writing with energy and intention to succeed. In doing that you're going to be inducing processes, you're going to be needing or paying attention to the need for discipline, self-discipline. Do you think it could be a sort of a secret recipe? Just focus on getting the writing sorted and do everything in your power to make that journey happen? As you're doing that, you'll also sort yourself out in many respects? A general package of benefit?

Alya: Yes, you can certainly say that. But to get to even that level it requires an understanding of the fact that this is what you describe: it is an actual process. So somebody needs to tell them that.

Helen: You just did.

Alya: That's knowledge, if you put it in a book. This knowledge has to come from somewhere. It's not inbuilt in a school leaver. From an Asian country or a developing country, they don't have that knowledge. They don't have the categories of knowledge that Western civilization or societies take for granted.

Helen: Yes, but Alya, you say we take it for granted, or we have it to hand. I grew up in England, in a family that was reasonably solvent. We didn't have serious issues with access to the basics of life. No political or community terror or strife. There was food, and if I wanted to buy some clothes, there was money for that need. Life was easy, really. I struggled *terribly* with this university writing process that we're talking about. Especially at undergraduate level. It was a car crash. I was smashing myself up and writing was the last thing on my list because I didn't know that it would smooth out the road for the myriad preoccupations I had of the social, or of learning to live. I had no discipline and if I'd known to apply discipline first to getting to the writing it would have been a useful process: a framework to live within, that worked well for me in that environment. What knowledge was I brought up with in a Western society that allowed me to know a process for university study? None! I've met plenty of people like me. They are still suffering in this manner of being blind. Nothing seems to have changed in respect of wising students up about this process approach that covers the whole of the university-student existential experience. You know, maybe because I'm creating this book you could say I've come through the other side, but that's many, many years later. The process was long and is ongoing. I can write now without stress but, like you say, that has been within a package of self-management. I'm forty-seven. So what can we say to students about their need to process quickly when you're saying it's a long process. There's an incompatibility there. I do think, however, that if I'd been told what this book is saying when I was eighteen, it would have helped me get a grip. To make a firm start. No one said a word.

Alya: The long process that I talk about is the actual doing it once you realize what it is that you have to do. What the issues are. When I say long process – if everything else is relative – for some students it is going to be *longer* than for others. A personal ability to handle all this material comes into play. So some people, once they understand the process, they can reasonably quickly, for example, within the course of a term – get better and their stress will go down and their world would be greatly improved. Or some people would take a year. Unfortunately – and I know this from many examples – for some it will never happen, not within their time at university. They will always struggle. I'm talking particularly about the three to four years of undergraduate level.

So there are two aspects of the process. One is the understanding of the process itself, which can be taught with some education in that respect. So if I don't know something I go to a book and I read about it. This applies to most subjects of life that you are interested in. The text that you're creating now would be that tool. OK? So at the beginning of university education it would be helpful for you to know these things. To say, 'This is what is ahead for you.' The teaching of the process doesn't need to take long for somebody who is willing. There is also the issue of willingness to be educated and openness, which is not a given and should not be taken for granted. We're talking about people who have decided they want to be at university and they are willing to understand what it takes to be good. That process doesn't have to be long. The process that will invariably be longer is actually *doing* it. You see, there are two aspects to this.

Helen: I found when speaking with students myself, when teaching academic writing – because there I am dealing for their sake with the inside mechanisms of succeeding at university – that speaking frankly and honestly matters. Not too honestly sometimes, but certainly with compassion and empathy for the idea that honesty about universities and strategies to succeed, to win, helps people to access successful action. It was very popular with students as a stance. They gave me feedback that they were desperate to know these kinds of things. It seemed to empower them. It was from that experience that I got the idea to write this book. The students appreciated hearing the inside of the matter. The hidden side of something. Do you think that universities could be more open and transparent about the difficulties involved in being a student? In order to make their life easier. Rather than assuming everyone's OK and they can get on with it no problem, so long as you know the library has fantastic books and the lecturers are great superstars, or whatever it might be. There's a need for compassion and empathy for human self. There's a need for compassion and empathy for the weakness and the vulnerability that we all present with, surely?

Alya: Yes, you certainly have a point in all of that. Universities can do a lot better at being open about all sorts of things. But my view is that the barrier there is universities being concerned that this will interfere with 'the student experience'. The student experience has to be good. Everyone wants to do very, very well in student experience surveys, which in the UK have become really important. The results of those determine *a lot* for the next academic year. So bringing students to university and serving them a hard lesson, because you are saying, let's be frank, this is what is ahead, might contravene what the student would perceive as an enjoyable type of university life. They were supposed to be looking forward to it as something good and something nice.

Helen: I think the enjoyment comes if people feel cared for and also are caring for themselves. Universities, I think, it must be stressed, are not there to do that job.

Alya: No, they are not.

Helen: But a book like this one has got nothing to lose. It can speak fearlessly. Set the matter in a wider context. A necessary undoing of silences about weakness, difficulty. In order to win.

Alya: It can. Absolutely. It's freedom of speech, which by all means do use. But the university is not and should not be a parent. At the same time, you don't trample on people either. In other words, it shouldn't make difficult lives worse. I think a university *does* have enough resources and ability to at least not make matters worse for a student, because you were talking about life preparation. I think there is an attempt to that end. In the fact that there are well-being departments and services in pretty much any university – certainly any British university of which I know something. They are called 'student well-being' departments. They are tasked with identifying these kind of issues. I would say the level of success is dependent on a number of things: one of them is a need for funding. But also the students' willingness to get themselves involved with such matters as deserving attention. You might think that that is easy enough to do, but actually it is not. Some students are really, really resistant to letting somebody guide them through matters that are not academic. For *a number* of reasons. Some are cultural and some are personal. For that there isn't a recipe that I know of, or I could trust, as saying, 'Well, we should be doing this? We're not doing that as a university well enough at this time.' For even if a university were putting in place services that were better tasked, better funded, it still doesn't guarantee that the people who need them most will in fact engage. That's a completely different subject.

Helen: Your point of do no harm is a wonderful one. If a university spirit is to not make matters worse that requires a level of compassion, and of understanding and empathy. But it also doesn't require the university to be the parent or the saviour because this is to enter into the drama triangle. But I think what I would like to do with the book is to emphasize to students that the university is not there and should not be expected to be there as anything other than a place where they can enjoy the *absolute* thrill of knowledge.

Alya: Yes, theoretically speaking, you do have a point. But the thrill of knowledge you also have to remember is accomplished through very, very hard work. Very, very hard study. And on that point, I think we may find that few people actually enjoy that process, or that aspect of the process. I would imagine it would be really wonderful to enjoy the thrill of knowledge, as you say, if it could be acquired freely. In other words, with minimum effort. But there is no such thing. Not in this country here. It's a lot of work.

Helen: As the saying goes, 'There's no such thing as a free lunch!' Yes, I see. If students are already paying monetarily, they will expect a product, a great experience, right? Not hard work. But then that enjoyment process that comes with the getting to enjoy knowledge – they pay for the infrastructure and context in which the process occurs with most support. Like the writing process is incremental, attaining higher levels of knowledge starts off and it feels like hard slog, but then you get into it and you get more interested and then everything becomes relevant. The puzzle of it all starts to fit together. Kinda. You can put things together and it becomes an art. Whatever the discipline.

Alya: It's true. If you are doing the right subject, that is. That is another story which I believe is very important. I think success in university is fundamentally dependent on your compatibility with the subject you actually study. So if you don't like the subject to start with, because your mother or father sent you to study medicine, because they are doctors and they think it's a good idea? You are going to forever struggle. You will not find enjoyment. You will not find the motivation. But you could go through university for the love of subject because *naturally* you love to learn about that subject. These are the people who stand the best chance for the enjoyment of knowledge, to take your phrase. But if there is a mismatch between the subject you study and what your interest actually is, knowledge wise, there will always be a struggle there. Very rarely any enjoyment. I do talk to a lot of students who say I struggle because the subject is boring. I don't want to do this. I do mean *a lot* of students.

Helen: Wow.

Alya: Not the occasional one. They tell me, 'I know I'm doing badly. I know I need to do better.' Some of them even know what to do. What it takes to do better. But at the end of it all, they admit that the main reason for this struggle is that because they hate it. That is emotion. That's not knowledge. With emotion there is nothing to do, because that's a given. It's very, very complicated. The truth is that success at university comes also from the emotional connection that we have with the subject under study. Not just the intellectual connection. If it was just the intellectual connection, we would all be robots. Potentially if it was just intellectually determined, everybody could do well. The cognitive domain is the most flexible of our personality domains. It is subject to education. The way we think can be altered by education. But the emotional domain is subject to nothing. It is an absolute given. So people who find the emotional compatibility, if you wish, with their subject, will do better. I wanted to go to university to study literature. I loved literature. Nothing to do with knowledge. Nothing to do with my intellectual ability. Hopefully, it was at a sufficient level required for me to pass an entrance exam to study literature at university. Therefore, I never struggled with motivation. I did struggle with subjects that I didn't like that were part of the course tangentially. But if somebody would have forced me to go and study a science, quite literally, I might have wanted to kill myself. Nothing to do with my intellectual ability. Just the emotion towards the subject.

Helen: I hadn't thought of that. I know this is something you're very interested in. The emotional side of studying. That aspect of emotions as linked to study.

Alya: I think it functions at the same level as everything else in life. Emotions operate at a very basic level. You like something or you don't like something. With people it's the same. We like someone, or we dislike someone. That is how it is with study as well. If you do want to study that subject, you're going to want to do better. If you don't want to study the subject because you don't like it, then there is no *engine*. Well, there's no *fuel* for an engine for us to create the power to do better. There is no food.

Helen: That's an aspect of the matter that I hadn't considered when I'm thinking or speak about the mechanistic side of winning the university game. We've talked about the process, the architecture of the planning, the devising, the taking care of oneself. These could all be seen as a sort of mechanistic set. A skill set. If you read this book, you'll get the skill set. It's mechanistic. But what you're talking about? It's something that is totally outside of that game plan.

Alya: I would think that what I just said now about emotional involvement perhaps should be at the top of your list in describing the process. Which is go to university to study a subject you actually want to study. Then by all means propose to students your recipe.

Helen: Yep, you're right.

Alya: But if you do go to university and study a subject you don't want to study? Then any list or aspects of a process to become better that you are going to propose to them through the book is going to be subject to the same trouble. So I would say that that is an essential thing before you get into any intellectual process to know how to study well. You need to be there for the right reasons.

Helen: Yes, I can see that. You are completely right.

Alya: Let's say you go to the cinema, OK? The process of the cinema is to actually watch the film. The film you are going to see is likely to be a poor experience for you if you do not like the genre. If you don't like horror movies, don't go to a horror film hoping to enjoy it throughout. You're not going to do so. You are in the wrong place. But if your genre is action films, by all means go and see an action film.

Helen: It's such a massive point.

Alya: Yes it is massive. A lot of people struggle with that before they go to university, and make a choice of study course based on a lack of volition, because they don't actually know what they like to do. That's a completely different topic and outside the scope of your book, but it's a very interesting point. It's part of the educational process: knowing what to do. I do talk to students who say, 'I came here because I didn't know what to do.'

Helen: So it's like a waiting room.

Alya: Talking of a waiting room, I do believe that the university has a major role to play in educating people to live life, in preparing people for life. I think universities should have that role. Because they are the top educational institution. From that point of view, therefore, we can't do a lot of hand holding. The more hand holding you do for students, the less likely you are to be effective in preparing them for the life ahead. I do say to students many, many times, 'While you are a student, you're OK. Because if anybody asks you what you do, you can say you are a student. So your life, while you study, is pretty much sorted.' When you are no longer a student then the question, 'what do you do?' becomes very hard indeed. Because now you need something *to* do. So I think for that process the university plays a role in preparing people for life. There's a roughness there in that process. Because preparing somebody for life is not necessarily, at all times, a pleasant endeavour as a learner. To be able to show someone what it is to indeed fall, in order to get back up, through hard work, which is what life would be for most people, not all – that is a rough process to be put through when you are eighteen. Well, at least in today's world. It would have been different fifty years ago, I would imagine.

Helen: You've opened up so many different issues. I'm looking for a way to finish this conversation between us, but that's really difficult because it has opened up all these interesting different areas which students will be experiencing, or thinking about, or maybe subconsciously encountering in the university. In other spaces of the book some of these will be mentioned. I think that last point you made about it being a rough process is a hugely educational one. It applies also to school education and how rough that can or should be if it's going to be educational. Often people complain about university experience being disappointing, or unfortunately not what they had expected. Unenjoyable and so forth. My own experience of being an undergraduate was all of those things. I came out of it, knowing how to think. I got something from it despite thinking I was getting nothing from it of any value. I could think. I'd encountered what thinking is in the university space.

Do you think – and this is my last question – any student going into a university will encounter *something* of value, whether they know it or not at the time? Is that *inevitable* given the space that a university is?

Alya: Yes, I do believe so. Indeed so it should be. For some students, the value of it all might come perhaps later in life. That would be the case if that particular value is affected by certain life events that need to take place before that value can actually reveal itself. For instance, how we handle a seriously difficult situation: emotional trauma or intellectual trauma. I think for most students the value will happen while they are at university, but perhaps in the second half. I'm talking for most students, not all. The reason why I say that is not just from my experience of speaking with students, but because I'm thinking of the process. The students would have to allow for the university to speak of them, of their abilities, through their written submissions. It takes a while before students can actually make sense of feedback. That will more likely occur after a while, in the second half of their time. The first half of a university course hasn't given them enough feedback on their work for them to understand how well they're actually performing. None of this – and I have to go back to that point – will make the process substantially better unless the student truly wants to be there, studying the subject. And *want* is emotion. It's not intellect. That to me is fundamental in understanding the problem. Also fundamental if you actually try to help somebody who has educational difficulties in terms of the process of going through university life. I think we have much less chance to help students who struggle if we don't appreciate the emotional impact – in fact, the very word that you use – of the experience. That universities should be *empathic*. That is your word. That only refers to emotion. Empathy is an attitude towards emotion. It's based on emotions solely, not anything else. Which is why some people are capable of it and some people aren't.

Helen: We started this discussion commenting on the instrumentality embedded in a possible interpretation of the title of the book and I find it very interesting that in everything that we've spoken about, we're not talking about instrumentality *at* all.

Alya: Yes. Quite possibly. I'm not sure how – is the title set in stone now?

Helen: I like the title immensely, although maybe it looks bad at first glance – instrumental – so the blurb – will – I'm going to have to make sure that it sends the right message. The people who are going to pick up the book for the somewhat instrumental sounding title are exactly the people, in my opinion, who need to read the book because it's not about instrumentality.

Alya: Well. Perhaps it will have a certain aspect of that. I would expect students to actually also read such a text wanting to know what to do, literally. And actually, students do come from schools with that mentality because this is what they know from schools: somebody will tell me what to do and how to do this. It's not a wasted scope if you were to introduce a feel or a sense of 'To do this is better than doing the other. Or, do this, it's better than doing nothing.'

Helen: It is instrumental in a sort of subverted sense that it's saying, don't forget that you are the powerhouse, you are in charge, you have to do the process and devise the means to succeed. It's not an instruction, but it is instrumental to say that. It's instrumental to success and self-care. To winning.

Alya: It is, I would agree. But understanding that you are, as you say, the powerhouse does not necessarily give you the ability to actually perform as such in real life.

Helen: But there's your process and your roughness. It's important to get through both, so –

Alya: That's right.

Helen: Thank you.

Alya: You're welcome.

5

A Fair Deal for Your Money?

*J*o discusses with me in this conversation the personal experience of students in universities, linked to individual gender and heritage. A difficult picture is presented of the university as inherently unfair, biased, requiring you as a student to fit in rather than to be appreciated for who you are. We talk about universities as representing diverse environments depending on which institution you attend and for this reason you need critical navigation skills and awareness. The ethics of all that the university fails to be – especially a failure to be equitable – makes for moments of sadness in this conversation where Jo laments the lost opportunities for student development and the perverting of natural potential that university 'righteousness' (instead of respect) creates. Universities are considered to be riding on their mythic status without having much merit, rather than actually working to deeply value students on campus. The picture is one of inertia and lackadaisical reliance on a given status quo, rather than care. The student fees you pay are discussed as forming dysfunctional attachments to learning and instrumentalization which can hurt you. Understanding good writing in universities and the art of self-education as political action comes to the fore in ways which can allow all students to stand up for themselves in the system that is a university.

Helen: OK, so I guess what I'm interested in talking with you about is your take on a student's experience.

Jo: Of the university?

Helen: Of it all. You've seen it all. You've heard it all. Especially you've heard it from their mouths. People like yourself with whom I'm speaking are saying what their true feelings are about the whole thing, in order that students can see from the inside. Rather than this miasma, this appearance that everything is lovely and everything is OK. From a professional perspective, you need to do that. Otherwise, like a colleague we know, you're going to get done over. This book is an opportunity to tell the truth.

Jo: I've been teaching in universities since 1994, for twenty-six years. That's half my life. Five different countries. In that twenty-six years a lot has happened. If I think about the kinds of students – because the experiences of students over that time are very mixed – the story changes a lot. So one question I would have is: Is there a timeframe or a place frame on this that is more important than others?

Helen: It's international and for any kind of student.

Jo: Across time you'll encounter different things and across university systems you will as well. It's really different to be a student now in some ways than it was in the early 2000s. My own experience of my own interpretation of people's experiences? They're likely to be mixed and coloured by each other. The other thing I would just try to keep at the front of my mind is it does matter how human beings experience this. Certainly the British university today, it really matters if you're white, if you're a person of colour, it really matters if you're a woman, it matters if you're of a normative gender, if you are working class. It really matters. All of those. It really matters if you are a parent or a carer, if you've got disabilities. It is a different experience for people.

Helen: Why in the UK?

Jo: I think it's true in the United States as well. It's also true in other places. There's a lot written about it in New Zealand and Australia. Less in Europe, but that's maybe because I'm not reading the European literature as much. Certainly in Canada. Because the institutions in these countries are predominantly white. A lot of them, not all of them, obviously, but the ones that are extremely unaware of their own historical whiteness, unaware of racism, unaware of ethnocentrism. They are resistant to changing it, really protective of normative, hegemonic ways of being. They use traditional paths of study and give value to certain kinds of education over others. You know in this country especially, there's a devaluation of anything but academic learning. The hierarchy of universities. One thing that was interesting when I came to this country as a student was I didn't understand the tiering of universities and the hierarchy of them. I didn't understand that there were these things called 'Russell Group' universities and there were these things called 'post 92'. I didn't understand how they were raced and classed and I didn't understand how your experience changed by going to one or the other of them, even though your education didn't necessarily. I didn't understand how that changed how people saw you. I didn't understand any of it.

Helen: What do you mean by experience?

Jo: There are often different kinds of *environments*. I mean the way the university system is set up. I moved jobs from one university to the next and all were 'post 92' universities in England. Then I arrived where I am now, which is a Russell Group university. When they gave me a tour in my department here, I cried. They were just showing me the things that you could use in the buildings. People in other universities didn't have access to that number of printers. They didn't have access to these kinds of offices. They didn't have access to this kind of furniture or to these kinds of administrative support systems. Some universities are just less funded in that way, and a student's experience of being in a place designed in a certain way for them is often different.

When I was at other universities – post 92 institutions – in the UK, the difference was less strong because they were more diverse. Here, even though we've got a really racially diverse student population and in terms of nationality, I know the experience of my students of colour at this Russell Group university, is – well the teaching staff are something like 95 per cent white here. It's significant there's a teaching staff like that and that students are not reflected. There is not much consciousness of what it means to have a curriculum that is based on all-white European people. The ethics that are taught are from the British Association of whatever. People are doing research in Egypt or in Thailand with British ethics. What is that? The knowledge that they're learning doesn't have any application really. It does in a general way, but they can't apply it directly because things like ethical practices and protocols are really different in different places. Because of this a lot of people feel very alone. A lot of people, a lot of the women I teach, especially the postgraduate students, suffer from male domination and patriarchal bullshit, as well as sexism. They learn about it.

One of the things that's interesting about your book is they learn about it, and they're deeply hurt, not only because of it but because they expect the universities to be someplace different. They experience it not only as the racism or the sexism, but they also experience it as a betrayal of this institution – the top university – that they thought was better. That they thought was different. Also working-class students are *constantly* feeling outside and constantly feeling dumb. I have had a lot of working-class women come in, especially at PhD level, or master's level, who come in and feel dumb and are made to feel dumb. Only through classes that aren't really classes – seminars that aren't formal seminars, classes outside of classes – is there an intellectual space where people can develop their language or speak in their own language, the way they choose to speak. So there they can get really affirmative feedback that 'yes, your thoughts are valuable, yes, you're learning something, yes, I could see progress in what you're doing'. That way they come to realize that they have a skill in being people.

I think that for a lot of students the university is experienced as a violent place in some quite significant ways, actually. In institutions that are just unwilling to face their own prejudices.

Helen: Why would they pay money to enter into an environment like that? If this book succeeds in giving them an understanding of what they're going to encounter, its other job is to give them the tools to encounter it, so that they pay money for a good experience. But my question to you is: Without this book and without that understanding upfront, as they somehow or other pay the fees, why would they do that? Is it ignorance or that the university is false in its message about what the university is about? A mystery.

Jo: I think it's probably neither. Maybe 'ignorance' is a word I would use only in the sense of lack of knowledge, not in the sense of people being so private that they don't want to engage. I don't think people see universities as places that are political. I don't. The university itself has a reputation as an institution of being a place of learning, a place of scholarship, of improving yourself. It sells itself, not necessarily through brochures for individual universities, but as an idea that has travelled down the line and travels through as an idea. A place where people are gathered who have learned and who have developed themselves and who can help other people do that. In the form of teaching.

I think what's interesting is a lot of my students at the undergraduate level don't know that their teachers do research. They don't understand the university as a place of research. Even in their third year, for example, in what's considered a research institution by its own reputation – we talk to the students about research and they don't understand that we do it, that we write about it, that we publish it. So the teaching and the research are quite divided. I don't think that students necessarily come to be taught by people they think have studied particular things. A lot of the first year undergraduate students come not really understanding that it's meant to be a qualitatively different kind of thinking. A different kind of relationship to knowledge, to yourself, to the world in relation to yourself. So part of the experience is actually learning that.

One of the demystifications is there's a gap between what they do at school and what they do here. A lot of people don't know what they're joining. I just think that they know it's what you do, if you have good grades and want a good job. They think that you can get a good job after it. No one teaches them about the relationship between higher education and labour. No one teaches them about the job market. No one teaches them about the differential value of degrees, depending on what kind of university you go to. And how those are also racialized. No one teaches them that stuff, yet universities themselves produce hundreds of papers and books about these things. It doesn't use its own knowledge production to act on the problems that it has in its relationship with students. That, I think, is a big betrayal. The university produces – we produce – research that says transitions are hard for young people, transitions are hard for older people, that higher education is highly racialized, highly gendered, highly classed. That it's a sorting mechanism, as much as school is, that it produces inequalities as much as school does. We have been producing that research literature for fifty years and little of that has filtered into any of the mechanisms, as far as I can see, of how students are recruited or how university is sold to them. So I feel like it's a betrayal and I feel like it's kind of a – I don't want to say it's like a pyramid scheme, but it has that kind of aspect to it. I don't think it's a deliberate lie. I don't think my colleagues really know. I think you have to study higher education to know.

Helen: I have to admit that as I started the work for this book, I didn't know. That shocks me because I knew something was wrong. I thought that more information was valuable and would stop people suffering. I'd seen so much suffering on the part of students, but I didn't know. What you're talking about now, I now know because I've read some literature recently that has opened my eyes. But, it shocks me that people who have the right attitude don't know – I think I had the right attitude – but I didn't know. So why is everybody circling around the university with this fantasy image, the myth of it as good? I'm in the game of education and I know that schools aren't good, despite the myth. But I hadn't applied it to the university. Why not? Why is that myth *so strong*?

Jo: It's fascinating. It's utterly fascinating. I think about my own university now. It doesn't work as an institution. Literally, *literally*, every single day it is held together only by the grace and the free labour of people who save students' lives and work so hard. I ask myself how is it possible this is in plain sight for people experiencing this and still it can't be seen? So there's something about what is the thing that people can't see? What is the myth structure that's been put up that filters that? I don't know if it's necessarily a failing of researchers like me or a failure of the relationship between research knowledge and public politics. This is published about but it's only published about in the *Times Higher Education Supplement* or in some of the blogs that people read about higher education. It never really makes the papers. It never really makes the news. It never really makes the headlines. It never really enters into families and schools. We don't have many people moving back and forth between schools and public places to talk about this.

It's still a small proportion of the population in a university at any given time. A lot of people are really antithetical to university, so you have people who are wary of higher education and want nothing to do with it. Or there are people who think it's either normal or great, or an aspiration. It's a dysfunctional attachment. There are some great articles about the university as a bad relationship. They apply psychoanalytic relationship theories to the university. These really resonate, in my view, about why people stay. There's so much hope in the promise of higher education regardless of whether people see it, or experience it, or not. I look at my undergraduate students and I don't think their experience *of learning* is great. They might have a good time at university. Except for Covid, of course. They're not having a good time this year (in 2020–21). This year is a disaster for them. I feel terrible for them, but I think they have a good time at university – those who don't have other struggles. But I don't think they really experience it as a place of learning first and foremost or that they experience their learning as something that really is theirs. That is different from before.

That is one thing that is different from before. Let's say fifteen or twenty years ago, I worked in universities where the myth of the university pertains: that you would improve your knowledge and become a better human being, improve your way of thinking in the world, learn something that mattered. Then you would serve, in the world, or as a better person. People got excited about what they were learning in a really personal way. It was still a myth then, and it was racialized, classed, gendered. But that general experience was much more something I experienced as an *actual* experience. Some of what goes on in universities that doesn't work anymore is based on that. The idea that you give people things to read or you read with people – give them a list of things that you think are important and can contribute to this development-of-self process: facilitate it. Increasingly you co-construct that with them. Then they do these activities which are not just instrumental activities, they actually have some sort of transformative effect on people, either epistemologically or ontologically, or relationally, or emotionally. You assume that you start a course and you end a course in terms of being in a different place. Then you're ready to go onto a different thing from a different point and build on that. That is how people teach now I think. It doesn't work most of the time. It doesn't work anymore, because a lot of the times people aren't engaging with knowledge in that way, either with each other or with themselves.

This is partly because a lot of them are working. A lot of them are working and not as part-time students. They're working when they are full-time students because they have to. They have taken out loans which has changed *everything* about the way this works in this country (the UK).

The kind of context in which loans were introduced here for education and the kind of place we were in, in terms of marketization, has made it a very commodity-oriented thing to attend a university. I have seen a fundamental change since students started paying. A lot of people really treat things instrumentally and I don't think students understand what that means and the impact it has on their experience. I know students don't understand how the university works. I know that they don't know that we don't control our own curriculum. I know that they don't know that we don't control our own assessments. They don't know that they don't know! They don't know how it works. They don't know, for example, that I can't give them extensions until they ask me, and I have to say it's not my authority. They don't know that if I want to change something in a curriculum at my university the process to do so takes a year and a half, because it goes through multiple committees.

Helen: A thesis in the book is that students can get through and enjoy themselves as long as they write well. Is there anything that they need to know apart from that?

Jo: That's also interesting because writing is an art. The idea that everyone can write well is a massive assumption about university life. In this country you don't have to learn to write. I think that's the most bullshit thing about this country I've ever seen, in terms of higher education. That students come into the university and they're just expected to write. That is *such* bullshit. Every single student, regardless of what discipline you had in the United States, when I was there, took a year-long academic writing course. We read, we wrote, every single week. People say to me 'Oh, you're a good writer'. I think, 'Not by my fucking molecules. I'm not a great writer all the time, but I learned how to write.' This is a huge betrayal. I'm really angry about this one because students are expected to come in and write straight off the bat. What? How unfair. My son is doing his exams right now. They don't teach them how to write, they teach them how to write exam question answers, and that's what my students do when they come in. They have to unlearn that. They come in A students or B students or whatever and then someone tells them, 'you're a shit writer'. That is so fucked up. Ask students to come in and then shoot them down for the way that they're writing and then not teach them because they're just *expected* to know. I'm so angry about the academic writing stuff!

Helen: This is the thing that it all hinges on for me in that if students could only appreciate that writing is the way to succeed and pay some attention to that particular act. Then they would be able to survive the academic side, get the certificate well without the stress and the drama, and go out and enjoy themselves for the rest of the time. Everyone would be happy. It would all flow very, very nicely.

Jo: Yeah, although if you think about science students and art students then that's a little bit different. They've also got to perform. They've also got to create. They've also got to be able to work in labs. There are other things they have to be able to do that aren't writing. Increasingly in the social sciences, they're expected to speak out. They're expected to listen in certain ways, to present, to design stuff. The call for diverse forms of assessment is also a call to engage more deeply with what students might need to learn to feel confident working in different modes. It has some good roots in it and has expanded problems for some students. Just like we can't assume people know how to write, we can't assume they know how to present and are comfortable doing it, right? Like what about people with social anxiety? We see that it's not just about having different forms of evaluation, but about how to create conditions that allow people to learn and practice various ways of being in the world.

Helen: Isn't it a space where they learn how to do that, though? It's a deliberate moulding and formation of their selves. From someone who doesn't know how to present, they do the presentation, they *have* to do it – and then they learn how to do it and by the end they are a great presenter, or at least better than they were.

Jo: That is the ideal! So yes, if that happens then that is amazing and that's a great experience for lots of people. What often happens is they are assigned presentations and sent off to work in groups and they present and then they just reinforce whether they're good or anxious about presenting. I think that's what happens.

Helen: That's not great.

Jo: I hope you talk to people who say, 'Yes in all of my experience, I teach my students how to write academically and I really coach them in performance and in presentation.' I hope you speak to people like that.

Helen: One of the conversations (here in this book – with Chen) mentions success they had had in helping students to present, despite the students' feelings of fear, but it sounded like one or two isolated cases where the academic had taken care of particular individuals who were clearly not coping with the format pushed upon them. Academics largely, in my experience, don't discuss the low level of transformative impact of presentations. It's not that they say they fail to transform students through such activities. It's just unspoken and not up for discussion. I suspect they find the whole thing unexciting and a bit difficult or disappointing. I don't know.

Jo: I will actually say that I do make a big effort with academic writing in my courses. My students do a lot of formative writing so that they get feedback on it, until they do the final assessments. By the time they get there they know what to expect and how to write it. It does mean grading all semester long, which is a lot of work actually, but I have them write small things. Because of that, the writing exercises I do with them, a lot of them do improve. Coaching people in writing works.

Helen: That's very interesting. Do you see aspects of them, of their studentship, their selfhood, do you see it forming because you, personally, are somebody who pays attention to the writing side of things? Is writing so powerful that it can help them in general?

Jo: Yes, if they learn how to write, what they have to do is learn how to think. I use writing, in my classes with undergraduates, in order to teach them to think at a different level. They have to learn to move from 'This is just what I think uninformed' to 'This is what I think having read something.' Then they move to: 'This is what I think after reading things and having to have to put them together in conversation with each other.' Then we get to: 'Now I'm going to be in that conversation myself and I'm going to look at people who disagree with aspects of that conversation.' It's a very standard view of that process of producing thought, presented to them as a step-by-step approach. It's hard for them. For the first one they assume it's all self-reflection and stuff, and then as they get to 'how do you make a connection between another person's thought and your thought?' it's not something that comes naturally for a lot of people. It's a non-relationship for people, so they have to learn how to enter into that.

That's what those assignments do. In one class they have to learn to summarize an argument. Which again is just basic skills. So what's the first thing they do? They give me a list of everything the person says. I reply with 'that's a list of what they said, which is great. Now you have that. Now how do you take care of what they're telling you? You know, what is, in ten words, the thing that they're telling you?' That's hard for people. And then, connect this to something else you've read and explain why you're connecting it that way. Connect these two things to some experience you have in your own life or something you see in the news or something you've seen somewhere else. And tell me why you're doing that. Then tell me what this other person says about it. So each of these things just makes them practice a different skill. Then they have to write about it.

Helen: Do you get to the apogee of the exercise which one could call where they think for themselves?

Jo: A little bit in that course. It's only a term-long course and they get closer to that. Some of them do achieve forming thoughts they can own as original creations, but it's usually the people who can already do that when they come in. A lot of them get a lot closer to that, which is fine. But what they do know at the end of that, a lot of them, is that they know *the difference* between what I'm asking them to do and what they did before. Having that knowledge is already a huge development in skills. If you can see what you're missing, you already know a lot more than you did.

Helen: Can you clarify what you mean when you say, 'what you're asking them to do and what they did before'?

Jo: If they come in and they've never thought about how reading someone can problematize what they think, or how reading something can expand what they know in a certain way, or they didn't know there are conversations that happen in texts. If they didn't know that there are conversations that happen, going on in the news or in academic literature or that things are wider than just someone's opinion. If they didn't know before that it matters whether someone's opinion is biased by certain factors of that writer's position or background: for instance you share a couple of papers on whiteness in education and one is written by a white woman from the United States, and one is written by a Black woman from the UK. If they didn't know that that mattered before and that it does matter to think about those positions and yet that you can't draw any conclusions from those positions, but you have to figure out what those positions mean and why. If they have some conscious appreciation of these subtleties when they leave, then that's already a lot more than they knew when they came in about how knowledge works. I don't think that my course is transformative for people. I would never say that you're going to come out at the end of this course as a critical thinker. But I do think that they can learn things that help them on that path.

Helen: Thank you. A final question. The sub-title of the book is *The Art of University-Based Self-Education.* Do you think it is possible for students to move from a position of dependency on the institution, which, as we've discussed, is betraying them in various ways? We've also mentioned that many students are not really interested in transforming themselves because they don't know that it's on offer to do so through learning about knowledge and gaining knowledge. Do you think it's possible in a three-year space, given the context for students, to learn the art of self-education in a university environment?

Jo: Totally.

Helen: That's good news.

Jo: I do totally think that. I think that is part of their learning about how to relate to institutions in general. I think it's going to be easier for students in critical departments, where people are already sceptical of institutions and understand institutions have problems. Where they're learning about social movements, it's going to be clear to them that people have to 'do it for themselves' or nothing happens. Students who are learning about social movement politics are going to be doing that anyway. Students who were involved in activism are going to be doing that anyway. A lot of students are activists. A lot are involved in decolonizing the curriculum and now many have been involved in 'no borders'. Universities are not border guards. There's a lot of students who are involved in ecological activism or involved in on-campus activism. Anybody in the student union, who is active there or anybody in the student clubs. Student societies are often really active spaces where students are reading, developing themselves, holding universities to account for things. There's a lot of opportunities to be involved in that sort of thing. But it's partly about the relationships. The grade-for-a-degree idea is a very terroristic one. Students at all levels, from undergraduate to PhD, are terrorized, because they are evaluated and those evaluations count, and have capital. So there is something about being able to delink yourself from that terroristic relationship with the grades: to understand it. Yes, it does matter.

You need to be strategic if that's what your game is. If you want the grades. If you don't want the grade, then it's a different game. Or if you don't care. But if you want the grade, then you have to be strategic about understanding the politics of the university and how it works. To understand that the stories the university tells you are not the only stories that there are and that regulations can always be bent and subverted. But you can't do that in a conformist mode or a subordinate mode to the university. You have to have a more critical way of being with the institution and see it in its complexity.

Helen: I think that the book is suggesting ways to survive that – what you're advocating there in feeling the power of subversion and I understand that we might say the point of the university is to allow students to know how subversion operates – but will they survive? You're talking also about an infrastructure that expects certain things, like the word count to be just so and so on and so forth. The subversion is limited, no?

Jo: Yes it is. But also I would say that do that and do the other things. One of the mistakes we all make, including students, is that we assume that if you're in the university you have to follow its rules to survive. That that is the only thing you're doing. Or an academic thinks, 'I only have this job and everything I have relates to it.' No. If you have to write a 2,500-word essay, write a 2,500-word essay and then you can also write something else for the university newspaper and you can also write something else for yourself, if that's what you want to do. You can put a lot into a 2,500-word essay that is you, that is subversive, that is good. Frankly the irony is of course that most of the time, the more you do that, the better grade you're going to get.

Helen: Exactly!

Jo: It's a win-win. There are so many doors to push on in the university that are already open. They look closed because they've got armour up. There are regulations and they look serious, but they can always be bent and they can always be changed. There are a lot of doors that people don't push on because they think they're locked, and they're not even there. They're just fantasies, as you say.

Helen: The shift I'd like the book to achieve – and your comments are extremely important – is that yes, students are kicking out in their societies and their union and the student paper, or whatever it is, that's kind of normal human behaviour, that's to be expected once you get free in your university. It's all this big experience. But the thesis of the book is that you can take care of the university experience at the level of what you are paying for, which is the certificate *and* enjoy yourself in the process. Not so much kick the door down, rather, insist on your voice mattering because you pay and because that solution there is the one you need. But not some pushy 'gimme', more a polite, persistent self-care full of self-belief, commitment to the idea of the university as about gaining knowledge because *for you* knowledge is personal power. The personal is political – the university has the infrastructure and the track record to deliver to you what you want and need to win, to succeed on your terms, which is *a relationship* with the experience at the personal level.

But there's a personal politics in the writing of essays. If you would only put your own mind into the 2,500 words in order to find that the process of doing so is highly enjoyable. Enjoy yourself in the activities and the societies, in the bar. You can also enjoy yourself through that mechanism of the 2,500 words.

Jo: Yes. There is also something as well about, when you say self-education, an opportunity for political education. The more students hold academics and administrators to account for the quality of their relationships and not in a consumerist's transactional sense always, although that has its strategic value as well, the better than is for everyone. We *encourage* students to do that sometimes because that's the only thing that universities listen to. But the more that you can hold the people who are teaching you and organizing your courses to account for things like the quality of their relationships and the depth of their own self-reflection and care, the more you can learn about the condition of that work. It's not just enjoying yourself. There's also being able to be recognized, for example, in a classroom, to be able to be seen. If you've got a really fucking transphobic professor, for example, and you're a trans person, or you have relations with trans people, you can sit there and feel, oh, I can't speak out. You know you might get a bad grade or this is going to be uncomfortable. Or, you can start that process of learning how to do that in society in a place that is relatively contained. It is society (the university), but at least there are conversations there in a way that there might not be in other places. If you see a syllabus that contains a really ethnocentric account of something – the more people learn how to hold those things to account collectively, the more the university is going to change.

Helen: With you they would be safe. What if they spoke out with the professor who's transphobic, for example, and it turned out that they were not safe to do so, and their grade did suffer, or some other prejudice?

Jo: And *that* is what is happening. The onus is on the university, the onus is on the academics for sure. I wouldn't say that this is the students' responsibility and the students are in that space. I actually think for them, in terms of your book, being aware that that is a space where these things happen, they need to go in being conscious about how they want to be in that space.

Helen: How they play it you mean?

Jo: How they play it with each other? Because it's the same question we have when we go into any space as human beings. What's going to happen on the tube, for example, when I hear someone start attacking someone else in a racist way? Who am I going to be in that moment? Students collectively, as well as individually, need to be prepared for that. My classroom is hopefully a place – it is not always safe for students. I know that it can't possibly be because I can't make it safe for them. I'm not always the same person. I want to be. I want to learn, but no classroom is ever permanently safe, you know? But I know that they need to learn in classrooms how to do that, to cope with dissent in a social setting. I wish we did more of this in universities and we're trying to in my programme now: to have formal spaces where people learn some basic strategies, learn to see basic patterns in classrooms, even among student populations. This they are interested in actually. Of all the things in my class that students find heat with it's things, like what do we do when there's a racist incident or how do we deal with homophobic language? How do we deal with people when there are different language divisions in the classroom? These are not comfortable spaces of the mind to enter, they don't enjoy them, but they're interested in them. We take what's going on in the classroom and sort of open it out. They sit up for that.

Helen: I'm hoping here, with our conversation and the others, that we are giving students a toolkit to open things up, and yet stay safe.

Jo: They need tools to stay safe. You need to give them tools to stay safe that don't mean staying quiet all the time. Staying quiet sometimes, as we know, is necessary and they need to be able to learn to discern that. When silence is – you've got a background in research on silence – best or better, wise or strategic. When a certain kind of silence is necessary in a particular moment. When also voice and whose voice matters to be heard. So, learning what it means to be in a certain position in the university. What kind of power do you have to make the university also a better, more enjoyable place for other people? White upper-class women, for example, learn to use your language differently and the university is a better place for everybody! What can you do to make sure that everybody is able to enjoy themselves? This is, maybe, a nice message.

6

To Enjoy the University is an Art

This conversation with Chen shows how curiosity is vital to studying well in a university, mainly because without curiosity the ways that the necessary art of self-education can occur are blocked. To be a university student is, Chen considers, a beautiful experience because of the time for thinking and reflection that this period in a person's life can offer. How you can make the most of that student experience is something we debate here because it is not an obvious thing. Chen emphasizes the freedom and flexibility involved in university life and these are both seen as connected to success: the business and busyness of students is discovery. Various useful academic skills, the art of studying in a second language and the vital role of writing as a discipline for achieving intellectual clarity are talked about. Chen sees university studying as a process: an incremental learning curve, requiring care. The conversation with Chen offers you ways towards the art of being and enjoying being what might be called 'a top student'.

Helen: I would like to ask you, how do you think students can enjoy university?

Chen: A student can enjoy university if they are curious. Curiosity is an important thing. Curiosity not only in the subject they study but also about different opinions. In challenging opinions. In discussing, debating, travelling. If they have exchanges or travelling just intellectually. Undertaking journeys through books, experiments, laboratories, methods, skills – they don't know to where these will take them, but if they are curious, they will go far.

Helen: You're talking in the context of one of the top universities in the world. That's where you work. I'm sure you bump into a lot of curious students there. But university students on the whole might be struggling to be curious because they've got lots of other things on their plate, in their mind. Maybe they go to university to enjoy themselves in other ways, like making friends, finding a partner.

Chen: I think curiosity is transversal to all levels of universities, income, academic ability and so on. You can find curiosity at every level of education. There are students who are not particularly curious at top universities because they're just skilled at passing exams. That's not being curious, and curiosity includes meeting other people at university. At university you encounter a more mixed environment than the one young people are used to at school or in the neighbourhood, or their sports club. That is an extra bonus. Especially now the university is quite multicultural and that again is at all levels, not only top universities. It depends on the country but in general you are exposed to different cultures, different trajectories of life. That is a part of it. Of the experience you can enjoy.

Helen: How and why is curiosity enjoyable and why is it perhaps particularly relevant to the university, if at all?

Chen: Curiosity is stimulated by a complex environment and the university environment is particularly complex. It is not a routine one as one would be more likely to meet if we started work at the same age. Unfortunately, much work is routine work and not that challenging, whereas university can stretch your curiosity and life in different directions. It is a luxury that people rarely have in life, outside years of study. If they don't make the most out of it, they will regret it. If they only have a narrow focus on passing with certain marks or ticking certain boxes without being more open-minded about which boxes matter enough to be ticked or not – discernment, rather than settling for a pre-set list – that is a shame. Those kind of intellectually challenging opportunities may happen again in life, but it gets harder and harder. Let's say it might occur again when you retire, but you may not have the energy to do it.

Helen: Well, how do students at a university ensure that they start their curiosity machine? How do they access this drive?

Chen: An example I give to research students, which is the kind of student I deal with most, but in a way it could be generalized for first-year students or first-time students of any level – is to have a butterfly period of evolution. It is a bit the opposite of being a caterpillar. First, the caterpillar exists and then they become a butterfly. The research student first has to be a butterfly and then they have to be like a caterpillar – feeding, digging in – to grow. A good thing about the butterfly period is you can fly around and taste all kinds of flowers you see. Therefore, for instance, don't choose your modules just because there is a list somewhere which is the standard choice or because there is some information provided about what to choose which says, 'These are the modules that are popular or that provide good marks', or whatever. Have a look around. Speak to as many people as possible. Go to the first few lectures for the first couple of weeks of all kinds of modules, maybe even in different departments. Usually, it is possible to pick modules in different departments. You will discover things you didn't think possible. They were not in your plan. When I was a student I changed my plan of study, I think every year, maybe apart from the very last one. I took models from different faculties and departments. Because I followed my evolving curiosity, one thing took me to somewhere else. It is open-mindedness that is particularly enjoyable. It may prevent you getting bored. Which is the opposite of being challenged and interested and having fun.

Helen: This open-mindedness thing. Universities are all of particular kinds, aren't they? So if a student is applying to a particular university, and they get in, they're entering with a specific mind-set adapted to the environment they've chosen. Is this curiosity that you're talking about independent of the environment of a particular university?

Chen: Oh no, I said my curiosity is subjective. This is a subjective attitude. However, it's stimulated in particular environments. Universities in general should be one of the most stimulating environments. Sometimes they fall short of it and that is a problem, but in general they are quite challenging. I would say that includes all universities. Because I know also in teaching universities which are not on the top of the league in terms of research, maybe, or in terms of reputation, still there are quite a lot of staff who are really passionate about their topics and their teaching, and they may have ideas which are not the same as the textbook. Therefore it is a great opportunity to be able to spend time talking or being challenged and challenging people who are experts of a certain topic. Who've spent already quite a lot of time getting into something deeply, whether for research or for teaching. As I said, it is a rather diverse environment, not in terms of age but in terms of ideas, cultures, origins. So that, in general, is a good opportunity to be curious and open-minded. University means universal knowledge. It doesn't mean specialism. No, it's exactly the opposite. University is not about specialism. Before you feed and dig in, you should have the butterfly period and get an idea of what the other flowers are.

Helen: So what has happened to a student who at university finds themselves feeling bored?

Chen: It may be a problem of the university, but don't feel stuck with what you have started. Generally there is a flexibility. It varies, but generally there is quite a lot of flexibility in terms of what you can study, you can adapt your modules. You can change a pathway in your degree. Sometimes you are even allowed to change degree without losing what you have already done. Go for a year abroad. There are quite a lot of things you can do. As I said, in comparison to other experiences where people can get stuck in life, such as work or even being responsible for maintaining a household, the university is quite an extreme level of freedom. You have a timetable, which is a few hours a week. Even that timetable, it's you who chooses much of it, rather than somebody else, and the rest of the timetable you organize yourself. Where are you going to have such freedom? Sometimes freedom is scary, and that is one of the most frequent reasons why students struggle. Especially in countries where you have a lot of freedom, such as the country where I come from. Other countries you are, let's say, spoon-fed a bit more, but it's a learning process. You shouldn't be scared of that freedom and you may make a couple of mistakes, but it's a great learning experience.

Helen: So is the best kind of student – the one that enjoys themselves most – the kind of student who can cope with freedom?

Chen: Enjoying yourself is something subjective. Some people can enjoy themselves for being stupid and some people can actually not feel they're enjoying themselves but be doing great work. So that is not really the point.

Helen: I don't understand.

Chen: You were saying – was the question 'Are the best students those who enjoy themselves'?

Helen: No, are the best students (the ones who enjoy themselves) – there I'm implying a connection between being a good student and enjoying, which is also of course up for debate – are those best students the ones who survive and navigate and thrive, the ones who can cope with the freedom of the university?

Chen: Yes. To some extent yes. Free spirits are those who flourish in universities. If you don't want to be free, maybe don't go to university. There is no particular reason to go to university if you don't want a degree of freedom, so in that sense, yes. But I object to the idea of the best students are those who enjoy themselves. Because in order to really enjoy the university, you have to get away as far as possible with this obsession with league tables and being the best. That is the opposite of curiosity. It's the opposite of enjoying yourself. You become stressed with being the top.

You should strive for excellence. Whether you are as excellent as everybody else, and therefore you're not top at all – it's better to be excellent like everybody else and therefore not be better than anybody, than be the best among everybody else in a very average nondescript arena. Interest is what should be more important. In the same way enjoying yourself is something subjective. So you can't compare enjoying yourself with the level attained by someone else. Each individual has to try to enjoy themselves as much as possible, not more than other people, because others may enjoy themselves by being stupid. So that is not the concern: to be the best or the one who enjoys most.

Helen: The curiosity that *I have* is whether the university inherently is an enjoyable experience.

Chen: That may be, it may not. I mean, you know, like all really good things in life, they are also a bit difficult. Otherwise they wouldn't be enjoyable. They would be boring. So there are challenges, crises and so on. Fortunately, universities nowadays are a bit better than they used to be at helping students when they get into crisis. But having some crises during university, some failure, it's absolutely normal. It's a part of it. Just like sport. Good sports involve fatigue, suffering, falling, injuries, defeats, disappointments. A sport that doesn't have all that is probably a very boring sport. Universities are more multifaceted things than sport. It's more varied. But again, if there wasn't a bit of suffering involved, there wouldn't be any sense of achievement at the end, like climbing a mountain. Climbing a little round hill is very easy, but you don't feel anything when you are at the top. The same applies to the university. I think this is something I learned by teaching. One of the first things. At the beginning you think you have to explain everything. No, no, it's not like this. Students should leave the lecture thinking, 'Oh I understood it but not entirely really. It's quite complicated.' Don't be scared of leaving things a bit unexplained. You shouldn't be obsessed with simplifying everything, displaying everything step by step which means dumbing everything down. You can leave things complicated. Leave some open questions and the students will then feel, 'Oh. I have to actually get back to this material, to this experiment, to this reading, or today's method and understand it a bit more.'

Helen: Sounds poetic.

Chen: It's the experience of many academics.

Helen: Ambiguity?

Chen: Yes, sure. Research is about solving problems and not about solving things that are not problematic, where there is no question. Then it's obvious. I mean, obviously it depends field by field, but even law as a discipline, which is actually full of seemingly mechanical set-in-stone legal problems, there are always different theories and approaches.

Helen: The university is quite a public experience, just like the sport that you mentioned. It's done in front of other people. How would a student best manage that aspect? What you're talking about is a life experience of challenge, but also of risk.

Chen: Sure. Well, students have very different characters. Some are extremely outspoken and they strive and look to be in the limelight. Others are at the other extreme. In my many years of teaching I've encountered students who were extremely shy or would ask you to let them not to do the presentation and so on. You have to have an individualized approach, but each of them should strive to get ahead. One of the best satisfactions in my teaching experience was seeing some students who were very anxious and who asked not to do presentations and then, in doing some group presentations and doing it quite well – I know that cost them a lot of effort – they were very satisfied in the end. They had never managed to do such a thing before. The same very shy students had to do some research and fieldwork for their essay and they were extremely scared. You have to help them a little bit more, to reassure them. They managed to do the interviews. Everyone starts from a different place. You have to accept that people have different skills, approaches, capabilities and so on. There is no one size fits all. All of them can have a nice experience in a way.

Helen: What about English as a second language? You yourself are a speaker of English as a fifth language. You know how it feels to conduct academic experience in a language that's not your mother tongue. Universities are full of international students who have to cope with English.

Chen: Well, it's very important to work on some basic academic skills. Note taking is hugely important. Even if nowadays people think they can record the lectures and seminars. But they can't write it for you. You can't just rely on machines doing the recording for you because they will never do the learning for you. The learning happens through engaging with the work via writing. You need to do some notetaking. That's a very important skill. It's very difficult to do it in a second language. It is possible. Learn some acronyms. Learn some ways to put down what is said with signs rather than words, and really concentrate. I studied in different languages and yes it was more tiring. But because it was a challenge I was concentrating extremely hard. I wanted to take notes of what was being said in the lecture. The same importance should be given to quick reading. Otherwise you get lost. Also academic writing. It's a bit different in maths and sciences, but some degree of precision is required in all disciplines. These are very important skills, but they are also extremely important as a skillset for work later, for living well. It's not something you do only for university. These are transferable skills.

You should exploit the university years to make the most out of the experience, because even if you don't stay in the field you've studied, it's likely that the language – English or whichever other languages you learned if you studied in a second language – that will be extremely useful in your life and your work, in your career.

Helen: The main thesis of the book, in a way, although the conversations dilute that to show how important other aspects also are, is that in all of this complexity, the way to thrive is to focus on the fact that the university requires you to write something well. That doesn't just include the way that you write it – good English, good grammar, good presentation, right structure – but also the content, of course, which goes back to your curiosity aspects. Do you think that's true?

Chen: Yes. Although I would say that the most important thing is to learn to be clear. To put things in a clear order. That's why writing is such a good exercise. I tell students to write, even if there is no need to write, just write. If you want to see me for an appointment, just write something before you see me. So I have something to read. Writing, putting ideas down, is a very important process of clearing your mind and clarifying what you want to say. I wouldn't say that achieving perfect English is the main concern. Sometimes students get so obsessed and scared of making mistakes they start using software or start to be tempted with plagiarizing. Good examiners will spot that, so it's an extremely dangerous thing if you do it beyond what is licit. I much prefer something written with some mistakes, but which is original and I can trace the direction of thinking, than something which is cut and pasted, or something that has been dealt with by somebody else in some way which causes much of the originality to be diluted. So don't be too scared about making some mistakes. It's very important to be clear, to be understood. That's completely different from being able to write well. Nowadays it's extremely unlikely you will get a literary award for university work. That shouldn't be your aim. Whether it is an essay, dissertation, writing done in exam conditions and so on. Don't worry about writing something of publishable quality in terms of literary quality. It can be boring. That's not the problem. But be understandable. Keep your sentences short if you're not very confident with the language. That way you reduce the risk. Yes, it will be a little bit of a childish writing. It doesn't matter. Just write your ideas in the simplest possible way. Don't worry about being perfect in English, worry only about being understandable. Follow your thoughts.

Obviously, if you're studying in the arts you may want to look after the style more than if you study business, or law, or economics, or science. But in general what I've said is true. Unless you're studying the English language perfect English should not be your main concern while you're at university. Make it clear to read. Not perfect. Not beautiful.

Helen: That is advice that connects to the task of writing. What you are saying, though, leads me to imagine that, in fact, more important than writing are the ingredients, and that essentially boils down, in the university, to thought. So thoughts, thinking, the quality of thinking, are more important than presenting the proof of the thinking, which is the writing?

Chen: That depends very much on what you're studying. I don't think there is an opposition between the two. You can have a great idea, a great intuition. That's fine but if you can't prove it, it's a bit of a problem. If you can prove something but it's obvious, not new, that's also a big problem. So, you need to find something that is interesting, useful, new *and* that you can actually support either with logic or with evidence. The degree of the balance between the two will vary. But I would say even in literary analysis you need – before you say an author is great or is a disaster – you need to have a systematic knowledge of what they actually have written. At the opposite end, if you are studying business, you need some evidence of why a certain form of accounting is particularly rigorous, before you can make that claim with validity and be judged well for your assertion.

You can also have a degree of critical approach, and intuition. You can't only pursue creativity, shall we say. That's not academic work. It is a balance and mixture of original voice and rigour in the face of the literature or data you are using. Maybe with philosophy and speculative philosophy? Some fields of philosophy – but even there rigour in the reading and analysis is required. So it varies very much depending on the topic or on a specific field. I'm dubious that there is an opposition between the quality of the thought and the evidence. Good academic work is strong on both sides. It's original, so some intuition. It is also rigorous.

Helen: In the presentation? The written aspect?

Chen: In the presentation. In checking for alternative explanations. You have a fantastic idea. Let's say about music. But test other possible ideas. Are there other possible ways? That's the way of being rigorous. Be honest about other possible explanations, other possible ways of doing that. That's where the rigour comes from. Don't just follow your own idea, which may sound fantastic, but by the end it may be nothing new because somebody else has done it already in a shorter way, so you just wasted your time.

Helen: Well, in every respect the thought and the writing is nothing without the reading and the reading occurs through the curiosity. But does it not then all come down, not to writing or thinking, but to reading?

Chen: You can read and write. In the olden days, before all this bibliographic software and so on, you'd read and then write a file about what you read. I mean on paper, with a pen. You handled a sort of little mini filing cabinet with pieces of paper for everything you'd read, with the title and the main ideas and you go would go back to that. Nowadays there isn't so much need for doing that because there is software that searches things for you immediately. But I recommend people write down what they read: the main ideas, their reaction and so on. That is a building block for writing about your own ideas. If you look at the manuscripts of the great philosophers, they wrote down a lot of notes. Hidden in those notes there are some fantastic ideas, because they were not just mechanical summaries. They included their elaboration. This is the same at any level for university students. It is one of the best exercises, especially for research students. The best dissertations are the product of a lot of writing.

Helen: That's obvious though because to get the qualification they have to present some writing.

Chen: I know it's obvious, but some students wait until year four to start writing and then they are in a big mess. They thought they had fantastic ideas but they never put it in writing and that's worth nothing. So I say from year one start writing, start writing. The worst that may happen is that you have a file in your computer. You don't even waste paper nowadays anymore, so you shouldn't be even sorry for the forests. Just write. It may be useful. It may be directly useful for the dissertation or it will be indirectly useful.

Helen: There's definitely an art to writing. I rewrite things. Students need to create their own way of writing, don't you think?

Chen: You learn by doing it.

Helen: My point is that some students are afraid to delete and edit their work. They think they're going to lose something. Sometimes I write something and

I think, 'Oh, I don't like that, now, how am I going to delete or edit this? Where do I start?' I'm not, though. It would be too complicated and boring to do that. So, I've developed a method of writing which very often involves 'moving on'. I just start again and rewrite it. That's often my way if I encounter big structural problems: not to undo and unpick the issues but give myself a fresh sheet, of course the content of which is very much informed by the previous version. I type quite quickly so I'm happy to lose what I previously wrote by moving on because losing time is not so much the issue. I create a new file to work with. I don't delete the original file. This is in case I ever want to go back to the old one and use any of it. I keep all older versions but it rarely happens that I return to those. Now, in the latest version, I have an improvement on the previous piece, a better version. It has a stronger voice if I start again. Of course that's not the only method – it's just the one that works for me. That's partly what you mean by 'keep writing', right?

Chen: People save usually different versions of their work, which is a good idea. Different titles for each file version.

Helen: At the same time you've got a process to get through and it involves, if you're a student, presenting your piece of writing for a grade. Then moving on to the next task, which is a written task or whatever, a laboratory task. It's never about your backlog of deleted or discarded files. It's just only about the performance aspect of presenting or submitting the final version.

Chen: It's not just about that. We are talking about a development curve that has value. I don't recommend people start writing the day before the deadline. It happens all the time, even with academic's work, I'm afraid. But if you, as I say, write as a process, it's much more helpful. It may not be written in a perfect form, or it can even be just power points or bullet points. This allows you to elaborate something which you can then put in writing in a better way. It starts the ball rolling. Something is better than nothing. It's better than an idea that you can forget.

Helen: Well, in the introduction of this book, where there is a list of basic advice – if that's the right word, and I don't think it is – it says that students should make sure they manage time well. This relates to writing. If you're writing something, it's a very good idea to first start well in advance of any deadline, then stop it, drop it, do something else. That way you've got an opportunity to go back to it with a fresh mind and read it. That's where you often find that it either stinks entirely or at least needs revision or editing, and can be much better. Sometimes you find it has worked out. By giving yourself that fresh mind to truly *return* to the writing, you improve it so much. You need to plan the time for this return visit to occur with a window of 'goodbye, see you soon' time between the two visits.

Chen: Yes. If you have the time, that's much better. No doubt. To take a break. It depends on the length. If you're writing three pages, I mean, it doesn't matter that much. The bigger the piece of work, the more important to have a break at some stage. Then you can get back to it with a critical mind. While you're writing you tend to think, 'oh, genius me, that's great, my idea is super.' You get very attached to it. You have to learn to sometimes let your ideas go. If they don't work, you see that. You know it won't pass the exam or it won't pass the scrutiny of a critical mind. It's good to think about it twice. Some ideas have better legs.

Helen: Well, that's what I mean by being afraid of editing or deleting. The art of writing.

Chen: It's very personal, writing. People can feel offended when they see the correction. If you're not writing in your own language, that's better, because you are used to seeing a lot of red marks and corrections. You're so used to it, so you're not particularly upset when you receive corrections. It's a process.

Helen: Some students might be afraid to lose the idea that, as you put it, doesn't have legs. Perhaps they fear they might not get another idea, or they'll have to work double the time and the effort to get a brand new idea that's an improvement. I don't think it's like that. I think there are so many ideas that we can apply to any given task. It's right to choose the best ones but because knowledge is so subjective, you could write something you think worthwhile, that your supervisor or the marker doesn't value very much or, that they admire.

Chen: Sure. Marking is not a perfect science. One set of marks doesn't mean much. You need the average across a variety of work to understand where you're at. Don't be too upset about sometimes being marked down and being marked up. But that doesn't mean you can write whatever you want, because obviously there are excellent ideas or ideas which are less excellent.

Helen: How do you know which are good ideas?

Chen: Well, it depends on the cannon or codes of that specific discipline, whether that is music or maths, or whatever discipline it is. If we think that everything is good enough, then we don't need the university. We still need to strive for excellence. Otherwise, don't go to university.

Helen: Having good ideas, 'ideas with legs', is that a talent or does it come to you as an obvious solution just because it makes sense if you are sufficiently embedded in knowing the literature?

Chen: There is a bit of talent and inclination and there is hard work. Among the excellent students I see there are different kinds. There are those who work terribly hard and they get there through hard work. Others get there through very good intuition and a decent educational background, even if they haven't worked that much. The same goes for the weak students. There are those who are weak because they don't work at all, and those who are weak because they are not original and are not critical. In general you need both intuition *and* rigour. Without that combination you probably won't do very well.

Helen: One final point. Thank you so much for your time today. This thing about rigour and originality and criticality, does that come from hanging out with other people in the university space? Can you get it by yourself in the library? Can you hang out with books alone and win, or do you need interaction with people?

Chen: To some extent you can hang out just with books and win. Yes. But that is not to be alone, to read, you know. There you are standing on the shoulders of giants. Of course you can, if you're a genius, just go back to yourself and try to formulate a new maths solution from scratch, but it's thousands of years so far of evolution in maths. It's much better to study what people have already discovered and get into the new problems. You can say exactly the same for any discipline. The more you are able to stand on the shoulders of giants by familiarizing yourself with the best work, the most cutting edge or foundational, the higher you can go to achieve. As for talking to people. It's fun, right? It's stimulating. Being stimulated and being stimulating matters in a university space. That's the route to the top marks. So by all means talk your study through with others. It's a good thing to do. Most helpful. You might not like what the others say, or you might be interested. At the very least it will help you understand what you yourself think and want to say.

7

Believing in the University?

This conversation is a tough read because it tackles believing in a university as idea and reality and finding it falls desperately short. The university may and does disillusion in ways which can cut us. Alex tells an all too convincing story of this trouble. It is not just that we might approach universities with some incredulity but, according to Alex, we ought to think deeper about how even this, somewhat light touch, might not be enough to save us. The violences of the university are not sugar-coated. We talk about how they are part of power imbalances in the world without accountability for the harm such inequalities – at every level of maintaining a rotten global status quo – create and enforce. This conversation questions the sustainability and wisdom of sustaining the university at all. To be involved in the university in any way is, Alex suggests, to be someone who needs to apply critical attention to what we do when we contribute to the university's continuation. You are, as a student, Alex says, being infantilized in universities when otherwise you would gain the potential to seek or contribute to solutions to global problems with confidence. Students are offered power through this conversation to re-envision what it might mean to be a university student and to know.

Helen: The title of the book as it started out with the publisher was *Enjoy Yourself! The Art of University-Based Self-Education*. It came out of the fact that I was very tired and annoyed at how little universities around the world take care of people, in the sense that although they don't actually have a direct responsibility to care for people's mental health, nevertheless, they definitely weren't paying any attention to the fact that the environment of the university is, as far as I'm concerned, violent and self-serving. Individuals get caught up in this horrible monster machine of egotism and lack of care, in which, by the way, they also participate, but I think mostly through ignorance of what they have got themselves into.

I'd heard over the years of people who had killed themselves on account of 'university sadness'. Other stories too. Constantly hearing things from all quarters and continents. I totally understand how students can feel really overwhelmed, intimidated and stressed about being at university. I just thought, well, this is all very unnecessary. There is so much wonder in accessing higher levels of knowledge and making your mind richer, deeper, broader. It's very useful for living to have better ideas, shall we say, or more informed ideas. So, it just struck me that students weren't enjoying themselves and they were paying all this money. Was there something that could be done?

Then the publishers suggested an alternative title *Playing the University Game: The Art of University-Based Self-Education*. The subtitle is very much me, because I'm an alternative educationist and it's all about autonomy, self-directed learning, that kind of thing. Yet, there was a sense in 'playing' which sounded a bit instrumental, although the other sense is where playing can be advantageous, even fun. I was thinking more about the project, and I encountered Eli Meyerhoff's book, *Beyond Education*.[1] There and through that book I encountered the kinds of perspectives that I believe you are interested to discuss. I was still very positive about the university as a project before reading *Beyond Education* and now I would say I'm ambivalent. Nevertheless, I notice there are still people who believe.

It's not about becoming part of the machinery, buying into all their ideas and their values or their lack of values and competing. The oil of the university system is competition and that can make people unhappy. Unless you are the ultimate winner and then I still question the morality of that person's or that institution's triumph. How do you play this game? The odds are probably stacked against you, particularly if you're Black in a racist environment or you're female in a sexist environment or you're someone otherwise-enabled, not fitting the picture of the 'right' model of who succeeds or challenged by forms of health difficulties and so on and so forth. How do you win *nevertheless*?

My question to you is what do you think students should know as they sign on the dotted line and pay a bunch of money?

Alex: That's a great question. First, I should say, I don't think of universities as exceptional in any way. That's the point for me. They are part of this violent, modern, colonial system and they are central to its reproduction. So, of course, they would also be violent, modern, colonial institutions. The thing that's different is they have a story about how they are benevolent, how they are serving the public good and how they are leading to social change in positive ways. What's important for me is *de-romanticizing* the university – and I know Eli Meyerhoff talks about this too – understanding that it's not really so different than other kinds of institutions that are more clearly and explicitly violent, that we might more obviously critique.

The other thing is that we are also our institutions. I mean this in the sense of those who are critical of the university but are in it. That includes faculty members like myself. Also students or at least many students. We are also part of the problem. I don't frame either critical scholars or critical students as somehow outside of the problem, which doesn't mean that these critical conversations about what we need to know are not important. But we have also been socialized into this violent, modern, colonial system. In many cases the things we personally want of the university are also violent and colonial.

I never assume that someone, just because they have a critique of something in the university, wants something truly different. Something truly different would require us to give up many of the advantages, the pleasures and things that we enjoy. I'm not sure for me the point of the university, even in a subversive way, would be to enjoy yourself.

My question is almost always, what are our responsibilities and our accountabilities? Who are we accountable to? In my understanding of this, we are accountable to everyone and everything, which is a bit capacious. However, if we're going to be in these violent, modern, colonial spaces and probably benefiting from them, even as we critique them, then who are we accountable to when we do that? What is it that we should be spending our time and energy doing here? While we do have access to the resources that the university provides that may be able to be redistributed, for instance, how can we create spaces for learning that do challenge in some ways the institution? Although I appreciate there are limits to what is possible. Even in the small pockets of the institution where people are trying to do things differently.

I think I just had to say that as a kind of initial thing. There's no romance at the university. Nor is there romance of the critique of the university. Because many of us who critique, we are also part of the problem.

Helen: That brings up a couple of things for me immediately. There are lots of people who no longer do work – as student or staff member – in higher education, yet are very interested in higher education level knowledge. They like doing that kind of work or being involved: going to a library, reading books, discussing, debating, writing. They likely attended a university at some point – to get a taste of the life of the mind? Although it's a shame that kind of activity is linked so inexorably and too often exclusively to university spaces. Now they imagine that there's a life of the mind outside of these institutions. They want all the good things that they enjoyed when they were locked inside the university system, with their member access privileges. The question is how do they get access to it? I'm someone like that. The answer is not easily found. The university owns the means to knowledge production, it seems. That is not right or fair for all people, right? That it is a members-only club and the membership is expensive. Control of knowledge production is so much centralized in the space of the university. It would be broader, better, richer, if it were more diffused across all minds and kinds of thinking and those minds were enriched by the university as resource. We, the people, own that territory, surely?

This is about students of the mind where-soever they are. There are students who might not want to take part in the university game, because they have problems with the widening participation agenda language as manipulative (see, e.g. Cahalan 2013; Wilkins and Burke 2015). They don't want to be press-ganged into feeling they are nothing or without value because they live a life *without* the university. Yet they feel or worry that they're missing out. They might feel that or they wonder what harm they're doing to themselves by not entering into the university fray. The trouble is, of course, that in order to know what you need to know to play differently you have to access the institution in which this expertise to advise and inform is locked. It's a bind. That's what this book is supposed to be: a key to a door that you can open and go through or not.

Alex: When I'm able to speak frankly to students, which is not necessarily the case in my courses, although *I try*, I think giving people as much information as possible is a good start. Then they can make decisions for themselves. I would never sugar-coat the violences of the university, the sometimes false promises, the cost of all the things that, even if the university does fulfil, someone is paying for it somewhere else. Seeing both how the university might be exploiting them, but also how they might be seeking advantages from the university that the university offers – I want them to understand *all* of that. Students see how they might have a critique and that might be important and they might be part of the problem as well. Then, having that information on the table for them to then decide 'OK, knowing all that, I still want to participate here, because the system we have is the only way to have the potential for a living wage once I graduate' or they decide 'you know it's not worth it. I'm going to pursue something else' or they try something in between, which is 'I'm going to be here. I'm going to be learning with very suspicious eyes and I'm going to be also looking for other places where education is happening' because it's not only in the university that education happens right?

If students are already here and they start learning this, they become very disillusioned with the promises that have been offered. I think that this disillusionment is actually a good thing, or a potentially good thing, because we want to shatter illusions so that we can deal with the reality of it.

My caution to them is always don't just have the critique be outwards. Have it be inwards, too. Why is it that we bought into these promises in the first place? There are two ways of conceptualizing the problem with the unfulfilled promises of the university. One is they should be fulfilling their promises. How do we fix this so that they are fulfilling them for even more people? Or maybe these promises were harmful to begin with because the cost of fulfilling them is a colonial violence that is exploitation, expropriation and ecological destruction for this thing to continue going. So maybe we need to shatter that promise and be seeking something else. That doesn't necessarily mean you have to leave the university immediately. I think once you become disillusioned you have other options. Some people do choose the option of leaving and wanting to build an alternative immediately. Some people want to stay and have the university see how can we use these resources, redistribute them for other purposes. Or some people say, you know, this thing is totally fucked up, but there's nowhere that isn't fucked up, so for the meantime let's stay and see what's possible, but not invest in the continuity of the institution. You invest in other possibilities. You don't necessarily know what they look like, therefore you wouldn't be seeking an immediate alternative, but your investment is not in the institution. You're just using the institution as it's also using you. Of course, you never really have the upper hand there.

Helen: What you're saying gives me a sense that the original title *Enjoy Yourself* – which was a response to the stress of students who I just wanted to be happy – is indeed flipping as this book is being created. *Enjoy Yourself* originally was a selfish, very middle-class idea that you should come to university and have a right to enjoy yourself in the context of a difficult environment. Yet talking with you, I feel this very idea of enjoy yourself needs to be smashed. It's not a case of you go to a university and you need to find time – which is sort of an original premise of the book – you need to find time to go down the bar or to the cafe with your friends and have a lovely experience and meet new people and the way to do that is to write well and quickly so that you don't stress yourself out and miss out on all those lovely, enjoyable experiences. All of this is about privileged people having the right to their privilege. Yet the university is, or should be, wider than that?

Alex: Yes. That's the thing I'm constantly struggling with. How to deepen our critique of the university so that it's not just – there is very much this nostalgia for the post-Second World War public university where I am located. A desire to return to that public generosity. Then I have to say, well, I mean the cost of that was the Cold War, which in many ways motivated all of the spending and it was economic global domination that allowed us all this money. Is that really what we want to go back to? That's the thing. This question of 'enjoy yourself', I don't hear my administrators say that so much about students, but they do have this protective streak about, well, we can't talk too much about climate change and about the potential for economic collapse and political instability, because the students will be *stressed*.

This is very infantilizing. The potential problems we are facing are profound. Protecting students from that or shielding them is not going to benefit them. It needs to be more like how do we, with them, prepare ourselves for the possible crises and even potential collapse of these different systems, so we understand how we got here. It was precisely by seeking the promises that institutions like the university offer that are inherently violent and unsustainable and now are sort of coming to a head. How do we say, 'This is how we got here, the solutions we currently have are generally efforts to restore and reform *this*, and maybe in the short term that's all we can do, but in the long term we might need to imagine and create together as we go, something radically different that we can't currently imagine.'

Yes, it will be difficult. Yes, many of the dreams that we have been offered will be shattered, but maybe they need to be. How do we learn to stay with this difficulty and hold all of this? To hold the complexities, the contradictions, the tensions that are going to be inevitable in this process. A process that we've already started and could very well deepen and become even more difficult to hold. I don't think sugar-coating that nor having students think of it as an outside problem, versus a problem that they are also part of, is helpful. I want them to see that we're all, we're all fucked up. We can also do something. It's not that we're all fucked up and so throw us away. We have the capacity for terrible and amazing things within us and we need to accept responsibility for the harmful things that we are a part of that we might be invested in and try to disinvest from them. So that we can imagine healthier ways of well-being for future generations of humans and other-than-human beings on the planet.

Helen: You and I have spoken about the issue of drama. I've mentioned to you that I'm very interested in the drama triangle in the context of the university and how to get out of it by entering into the winners' triangle. There's a formula in the book, if you like, of not being in the drama of the university. How do the students exit that? So they can, as you say, take responsibility? Exiting this drama triangle where you have the three connected positions of victim, persecutor and rescuer is to take responsibility, state your vulnerabilities and take care of yourself. That's the winning play in the game. OK. But this is all in the context of a difficult truth to do with taking responsibility, which is painful for lots of people.

I have personally reached a point where I no longer desire to believe in bullshit and there's *so much* of it. The university is a huge manufacturer, perpetuator, lover of bigging themselves up, in terms of how rich they are, how well placed they are on the league table, how many people they reject for admissions, how prestigious they are, how fancy, lovely, well-polished and clever the people that attend the university are. This kind of thing. Of course, it's not 'true'. There are so many different people at the university. Like you say, we're all fucked up. But very often to only a somewhat degree, with lots of positive features and great talents. That's the truth. A super polished, perfect, unflawed version is not the truth at all. If we could just be a bit more honest with each other, a bit more transparent about that mixed profile, instead of believing we need or are expected to be perfect. Then we could not only take responsibility, we could have some *really* good conversations. Potentially of a qualitatively new kind, which are much better conversations than some of the ones that currently circulate where avoiding truth seems to be an ultimate goal.

This book is from the inside out. All the conversations here are people speaking their understanding of truth about the university for the sake of students – an attempt to have those kinds of conversations about being a student in the university. Like you say, students should be informed. I'm not seeing very much information going their way before they enter and discover the cracks in the facade. Is there a desire for honesty? What do you think about the idea of that desire in the context of being a university student? They don't want it? Or do they?

Alex: It probably depends on the student. I think among the hardest things for people to hear and encounter are that their hopes and expectations of something do not meet their dream of it and investment in it. Some international students are spending tens of thousands of dollars a year, or their families are, and sometimes have sold everything they had to be able to come here. Then they encounter the reality that not only is it not as they'd pictured, which they themselves generally figure out quickly enough, but if they take a class on critical approaches, they might start to realize even their desire to come here is part of this modern colonial imaginary. It's not just that the university is taking advantage of their position in the hierarchy of that imaginary. I have to ask the students, 'Well, why is it that you chose here?' and in many cases it is something like 'The ranking' and other things that are part of that same grammar: competition and advantage. Those are very difficult things for people to grapple with if they have invested so much. Not only financial investments but also emotional investments in the promises of the university. It's easier for people to be honest when the problem is just *out there*. It becomes a lot trickier once we start to see how embedded we also are in it. Part of that is because we, in Western society, have these binaries about 'you're good, or you're a bad person'. Like you said, this drama of you're the victim, the villain or the rescuer.

In not seeing we have this full scope of humanity in us or that our existence isn't defined by what we say and what we do, we don't really know what it means that we are intrinsically worthy. We only know, 'I'm as worthy as my college degree, I'm as worthy as a job, or as good as the economic value I produce.' If you question our harmful investments people start getting into a trap of worthlessness.

People tend to think we are either 'more' or 'less' than others. But this approach goes against our individual and collective well-being. This is the hierarchy of Western society, where you're either on top or you're on the bottom. If you're on the bottom, generally you think you need to be on the top and let's just flip the script. You change who is in which position. However, what doesn't change is the binary structure. How do we get to a place that's neither more than nor less than; that's not worthlessness, it's intrinsic worth. You don't have to prove anything to anyone. But we don't know how to think of ourselves that way. We only know how to measure ourselves by these economies of the modern colonial world.

Once we start to have these difficult questions about our investments, our being part of the problem, it can really lead people down a dark path. If we don't say, 'You know what, there are other ways' we can become lost. It's not that we then *appropriate* other ways from elsewhere, alternative spaces to this grammar like Indigenous communities, but these communities remind us there are other ways of dealing with the full spectrum of humanity within us and when growing up. Accepting responsibility for the harm we have done is trying to imagine and create something different, never assuming that we're going down the right path. That's the other thing that sometimes happens with alternatives: we see a replacement for the system we now have, as if it's a ready-made idealized replacement. The reality is that most replacements are also flawed. Not only because that's just how humans work, but because we're imagining the alternative from within this system, even if we have a critique of the system. We're so deeply imprinted by this stuff that the alternatives we imagine might have something different, but many things will be the same because of the conditioning with which we handle it.

So how do we work with all that complexity? We're not well equipped to handle complexity either, so I think the honest conversations are incredibly important, but they need framings. To understand just how difficult it is to truly be honest. To hold all of this complexity and complicity and the depth of the challenges that we face and not to feel overwhelmed. Not to seek the feeling good that you were talking about but to seek other sources of healthy well-being and other sources of joy. How can we joyfully learn to make fertilizer out of our bullshit that's not only the bullshit of the university but also our own bullshit? It's all to be determined.

Helen: What you say reminds me of *Silence in Schools* (Lees 2012) I wrote, because you mentioned being more or less, as in opposition. Such binary approaches in schools operate as labels of the system and remove people from the possibility of personal responsibility for learning and study: a child is clever or stupid, good at a subject or bad, well behaved or naughty. The solution, according to that book, is for schools to utilize silence as a chosen experience. The silence they use removes binaries. It offers an experience, albeit momentary but that's enough to know something new, of neutrality. In that neutrality comes personal empowerment and this can lead to taking and desiring responsibility.

Do you think that one of the ways students can approach the university as a complicated and difficult environment and gain a path towards owning control of their own well-being and study agenda is to use positive, chosen silence? Through forms of quietness, meditation or mindfulness? Doing this to achieve a position of intrinsic worth that you highlight and to deal with the onslaught of technology, social media, stimulations within the grammar of Being you mention?

Alex: For me it's not about having one specific form to interrupt the intellect. We've overstated the importance of the intellect in Western societies, which is only 20 per cent of the world in our lives and things that happen. Yet we consider the intellect as if it were everything. There are a cacophony of perspectives and information because of technology and other ways of accessing and sharing information. It becomes overwhelming. There's no coherence. On one level silence and other approaches for interrupting the intellect challenge the hegemony of this idea of a single narrative that can hold us all together. This narrative is usually held tight by those in power, including the university. I think already the epistemic authority of the university is being challenged. While there's potential there for something very important to come out of an interruption of the knowledge hegemony, what happens is that, of the cacophony people can't make sense, they selectively consume the parts they like, whether or not it's coherent. It doesn't matter whether there's accountability. You just take the parts that are convenient for you: what makes you feel good if you're an individual or, if it's an institution, the most profitable aspects. I don't think we can rely on the intellect, even if we wanted to, as a centring practice or to hear something else.

Meditation can be a centring practice. What I find often is that the incorporation of things like meditation into mainstream institutions is generally instrumentalized for people to be well in those institutions, for the institution to just keep going. It's a case of 'How do we make you more functional for this dysfunctional institution?', as opposed to 'How can this process help us see how crazy this whole thing is and potentially become disillusioned with it?' Whether or not these practices lead us somewhere different depends on how we frame them and how we approach them. I certainly agree that there is a need for something beyond just reading textbooks. There's great value in reading the critique written in these books. But, number one, the attention span is not there. Number two, critique can only do so much. Every critique is situated and limited, and has gifts of course, but they can't prescribe for us what needs to be done. We have to be able to *discern*, depending on our positionality, depending on our context, what, now that we have this deeper information and deeper analysis of the problem, we are being called to do. That's going to be different for me and you and for my racialized colleagues and everyone else.

Helen: When I think of what the university is good for – in the profound sense of the word good – what comes to mind is that it can be a very unique experience of sanctuary. In this sanctuary students are possibly protected from the requirements of holding down a job, paying a mortgage. For some their life outside the university might not be of sanctuary, for sure. Also, in and of the university there are forms of violence, symbolic and otherwise of which we have already spoken. It's not an innocent place, and far from it, alas. However, some corners there are in which one can feel safe, right? Entering into a quiet library, strolling silently across the often beautiful or interesting campus, sitting and pondering or reading in a cafe and just thinking about ideas, discussing ideas with friends, going to a stimulating lecture. All these things that the university can do. There are elements of sanctuary embedded in those experiences potentially. Is that something that you think is a value in combining the possibility of the radicality of choosing silence as a non-binary space, with the fact of the university is good for some things, and maybe sanctuary in company of forms of silence, stillness, calm is one of them? And out of that, can ideas arrive? Free and on their own terms and not on the university's terms?

Alex: As you say, for some people in some circumstances, the university can be a sanctuary. I know that. That's true and not only for privileged people. But I do also know the great cost of the university for many people, especially systemically marginalized populations. Every single day that they are on campus, they encounter racism from their colleagues, racism from campus police, racism against faculty, from their own students. Of course, for students as well, as you say, people's lives outside of the university are in many ways not optimal for accommodating peaceful, easy university study. They are sometimes working multiple jobs, have families. They have these realities that maybe the university itself serves, during those moments in the classroom, as some kind of sanctuary. Or maybe not.

As long as we're here, we need to find ways of keeping sane but understanding that the institution itself is *insane* and there's no making it sane. There's no justifying at the end of the day the cost of sustaining it. For now, the university stands and I'm not suggesting we tear it down. I know some people are. I'm not suggesting keeping it going longer than it needs to be either. So my approach is to ask, 'How do we not tear it down pre-emptively, but not try to keep it going for its own sake, because maybe something else is waiting to emerge and we don't necessarily know what that thing is?' You can't project these fantasies about what it could be because you are always asking, 'How do you actually allow the thing to emerge and have discernment about whether or not it's a wiser possibility, or if it's more of the same, or a different, bad possibility?' All of those things are possible.

There are ways of making pockets of the university more liveable. I think there's many ways of reducing harm in the university. We could be focusing on these, but I'm wary of people confusing what I think of as harm reduction of a system that can't be reformed, and their thinking that's the whole game. For me harm reduction is part of it, and it's very important to make life more liveable for those who are here. But it's not the solution, it's just one part. The other part is how do we loosen our attachment to this thing 'the university' so that we can allow something else to emerge? How do we learn how to learn differently? Sometimes it's about bringing other knowledges into the university from different knowledge systems. But what generally happens in those cases is that it's very selectively consumed, or appropriated and not really valued on its own terms and with its own context. Can the university be a space for the *interface* of different knowledge systems? I think it's worth trying. As long as we have them. However, I'm cautious. I have heard stories about Indigenous knowledges being brought into the university and being consumed in ways that are very harmful. It doesn't mean we don't try to see what might be possible, but we don't assume that it's going to go well, or that good intentions are enough to make something different happen.

Helen: We need to accept the reality of why so many students want to go to university: because the system is the system and they have the dreams that they have and they also have requirements for certification. That's the reality of the job market and so on. We discussed what kind of environment they are entering into. So is the solution for students, as I thought, but you may disrupt this, to go in with the attitude – and there you find this idea of the sanctuary space – with an attitude of *using* the university? They go in and they work out how they can use this space to their advantage, including one might hope, but it's not a given, the idea of using it to their own *and* others' advantage. How can the university, as a resource that they're paying for, be used fully and best by students?

Alex: 'Use' can mean so many different things. Plenty of people will use it to perpetuate the system and to see advantage within the system. That's understandable, given the system that we have. My own interest is the specific kind of use of the university where we use it to be able to face its possible end and the end of the systems around it, so that we can have healthier, less violent ways of living together. I'm personally not overly focused on how students can use it for the sake of advancing their careers. Although that is understandable. I think all of us do that to some extent but to 'use' the university with accountability, we have to understand that we are also part of the problem. Our desires to use it in this way, or that way, could very well be colonial desires of exploitation and domination of others. That, as you said, is an honest conversation, a very difficult conversation, to have. For those discussions one needs to bring a mild version of that conversation to general spaces, not a very deep one, because there will be huge push-back. If people understand they might be colonial in their approach, they either just dismiss it and say that's bullshit, or if they see it has some truth to it then they get very angry. Unless they're already looking for it. The critique and the pathways out need to be available for people who are looking, but advertising it is dangerous: it's not a very popular idea for either faculty or most students to encounter.

Helen: It's a desire to think, *if you want*. This brings me to my final discussion point which is to do with science. You spoke about Indigenous knowledge entering into the university space. Academics worth their salt, one could suggest, are aware of the power of science and where its power likely comes from. They have pondered its origins and nature, within their discipline. Also perhaps they have considered the race and gender of its 'source', in a Western world at least. But it's bigger than that. A certain kind of science is now a force that determines whether knowledge is valuable or not. You, like me, seem very interested in the possibility of other kinds of knowledge, other kinds of scientific enquiry, on new or other terms. If these other kinds of knowledge are not classified as knowledge in a space dedicated to forms of knowledge such as the 'scientific university', how do you win that game of knowing and thinking differently? You will always be so-called unscientific because you don't comply with the rules of knowing as per the university's standardization of knowing. Which equates to being unacceptable and even plain wrong. An uncomfortable position to have to hold and defend oneself against having as a label.

Alex: There's multiple games happening at the same time. There is the game within the rules of the university, and then there's the bigger game which is that we may not have a university at all. So if we're talking about the first one science needs to be more modest and not assume it has all the answers. We need to recognize that Western science is extremely important, but not universal, and equally understand that other knowledge systems are also important, but not universal. It's a very difficult task because the notion of science as universal, as objective, as the height of human intellectual development, is so deeply ingrained, not only in scientists but in many of us. Interrupting that is extremely difficult. There might be some recognition that we need to consider these other things that the humanities or other knowledge systems can offer, but at the end of the day, those are all in the service of science. It's extremely difficult to have people understand that different knowledges are all situated in a particular context. They all have a gift. They all have limitations.

I don't know how to interrupt that. If your way of thinking is framed by this hierarchy, someone challenging that hierarchy doesn't necessarily interrupt your way of thinking. We can say this is not just a rational or intellectual problem, it's a problem of how we relate to others. If we really think of ourselves, this includes scientists, as good people who are not racist and whatever else, then we would have to say, 'OK, other people's knowledge systems must be *equally* valuable.' How do you not have that as a starting point? I don't know, but we generally don't. The diffidence may be more of a dissonance. If you really want to work with Indigenous people then you would need to have as a starting point a true equality of knowledges. We're very far away from it. It's not just an intellectual problem.

It's not about *explaining* this to scientists or others. It's challenging their investments too and their assumptions about their own intellectual supremacy. How do you say, 'Sorry, you're not better than or less than anybody else'?, which is usually the assumption we make. People often think if you are critiquing science then you're totally trashing it and then *they're* worthless. No! It's just we're all on the same plane. It doesn't mean we do the same thing or that our knowledges have the same uses that are equally useful in every context. No. But to say we're really equally worthy, for the people who are currently feeling 'more worthy', it feels like a demotion. It's a case of dealing with desires and investments and the pleasures that they get from the superior status. It's not just describing that here's the history of science and how it's violent. That's important, but dealing with their investments –

Helen: Construction?

Alex: Yes. Of the self. Whether you're in the university or not, having these kinds of conversations is difficult right now. But I really feel like young people today know that there's a lot of bullshit that has been normalized and yet, no one wants to talk about it. So they're just sort of maybe playing along or not, and adults are saying, 'let's protect them and not talk about these things.' But really, I think that's just us protecting ourselves because we're scared to talk about it so we don't talk about it, but the younger people are more like 'the gig is up you guys, we know this is a scam, so . . .'.

Helen: Thank you Alex. It's been hard to hear we all need to stop working so hard at being 'more than' other people, but I think you are right. It's a negative drama. Students deserve a better story to believe in.

8

Universities Are Us

In this conversation we see, warts and all, from the managerial side of the university fence and we are not impressed. As a person coming from a working-class background Gurpreet believed strongly that the university was a good thing and then – discovered how many false promises there are. University teaching is talked about and that, as a student, you need to serve yourself because there isn't effective educational care for you on the part of the university. Students are advised by Gurpreet to get their head around university drama and university-based personal drama to avoid being sucked into dysfunctional dynamics. We discuss here whether universities cause illness and whether they are benign, agenda-free, fair environments. The answer to the first is given as 'maybe' and to the second 'definitely not'. The unfortunate problem of power imbalance is mentioned as a key problem, causing also in the bigger picture social injustice. Gurpreet advises any student to avoid 'divide-and-conquer' atmospheres within a student cohort and overcome the university's failures by being together and for each other. With a strongly grounded rationale locked onto Gurpreet's sense of the injustice that students are not being properly served, students are advised to approach universities-as-businesses with a consumer mentality.

Helen: What advice, Gurpreet, would you give to students thinking about going to or who are in a university? So they can have a good time, in whatever way.

Gurpreet: Universities are what you make them. They are really not about just the academic side or all the wonderful experiences you think you're going to have. It is very much self-based education. It's what you make of it for yourself.

Helen: Why do you think that is? I mean, students are often paying a lot of money in one way or another to study. Shouldn't the university do something for them, instead of them having to do all the 'self-education'?

Gurpreet: I'll go through a few things.

Helen: From how you say that, do I sense there is some emotion in this?

Gurpreet: There is. I know you wanted to look at universities and the kind of environment that they are, and I typically have always had a very idealistic view of higher education. That comes from being the first one in my family to go to university from a working-class background. So I had a really idealized view of higher education. It was something really to aspire to. I was fortunate enough to have a handful of really good school teachers. So, for me university education has always been an ideal and an aspiration – to transform people's lives.

But from my university experience and from my school experience, I suppose I can say that I've only ever had an excellent and inspirational experience as a student from a minority of academics and school teachers. Then from my experiences working as an academic, I would say now that I've only worked with a few inspirational and student-centred academics. It is a minority. On the other hand my experiences in my role as a university head of department have been that I have had lots of disappointing experiences with student complaints. I've had to deal with academics who, unfortunately, are really self-centred, rather than student-centred. My passion and why I went into education was because I wanted education to do for others what it had done for me.

If students take on that really idealized view that I naively had of higher education, it can be a disappointment. Students need to make of the university what they want it to be for themselves. It isn't going to be a case of 'the world is your oyster'. Students need to understand what universities do offer and what they don't offer. What are their responsibilities and what expectations they need to have to be realistic.

Helen: You've mentioned the disappointing people. As members of staff in any workplace, over time, you get to learn who's doing a good job, who's not doing a good job, who cares and who doesn't. These are work colleagues. You come into an understanding of that scene slowly in a workplace, wherever you are. Whereas students are not that connected to academics. They're not there for that long either. It might take someone three or four years to understand in a work environment who are the goodies and who are the baddies, whereas students aren't really going to get access to that knowledge. They understand blindly, perhaps about the people side of things and possibly get emotional because they don't understand. Has that been your experience?

Gurpreet: Some of the students I've worked with, because they have been student teachers, have actually understood education better than the typical university student. It comes as part of their knowledge base to understand what good learning, teaching and assessment are. Those students are really quite disappointed with the university education that they encounter because they know that they're doing a really good job in their classroom at school, whatever, but they're not getting that calibre of education from universities and they expect *so much more.*

For example, when I was a senior teacher in a primary school, I was responsible for teacher training and staff development. When I joined my first university as a member of staff, I couldn't wait to see the wonderful university transformative staff development that I would experience. My first day at my first university was Staff Development Day. It was really underwhelming. I couldn't believe that was a university faculty staff development day because we had been doing much more innovative, inspirational and differentiated staff development for school teachers.

Universities are very traditional in so many ways. Differentiation, for example, is talked about all the time in schools. But it is not discussed at all in universities and we are not differentiating so that really talented students progress from undergraduate to master's level study to doctoral study. There isn't that differentiation and that high calibre education in universities that school pupils can experience if a teacher makes an effort to provide an individual personalized approach to education.

Helen: It's almost as though the university doesn't teach. Even though students are paying all this money to get taught – at undergraduate level anyway. If you compare it to a school environment, you've got efforts for differentiation, special education needs attention, assistance to help where assistance is needed. All kinds of technologies of contribution to the possibility that somebody might be able to access and enjoy the learning content. Whatever we think about the pedagogy of all of that, that's another matter. But at least schools are aware that each individual student comes to it with a set of learning-relevant baggage and attending to this is important. Universities don't seem to care about any of that.

Gurpreet: No, not at all. I know that there is such a lot that schools can learn from university education, but there is an awful lot that universities can learn from really innovative schools. I'm talking about some of our best comprehensive secondary schools in England. Yet there is a real arrogance and reluctance to do that, because the school is deemed inferior by lots of academics. Our university students are often coming from a much better experience being in secondary schools and also better facilities and more up-to-date technologies than they have in the university. I suppose it's a little bit like my first day working as an academic that I just mentioned. I really expected something special. Students, particularly younger students who come from secondary school at eighteen into university study, they expect when they step up an academic level from level 3 to level 4 that they'll have their horizons broadened and the bar will be raised. That is a disappointment I think, for lots of students.

Helen: What about pedagogy? Is there a way to teach in a university that you think is best?

Gurpreet: I believe in andragogy. University academics have got a lot to learn from the andragogical approach. One of my criticisms of some of the academics that I've worked with, probably because lots have been teacher educators, is that they teach in a very didactic pedagogical way. An andragogical way is more appropriate for adult learners. That is an issue. Andragogy is too little known and not sufficiently understood.

Helen: You're talking about a huge paradox, a mess. A paradoxical mess, because universities are too arrogant to teach like schools, but teach like schools, in a way fit (and that's contestable) for children. Students need to help themselves because universities don't help. Andragogy is a form of pedagogy which involves students finding their own feet and making their own way, obviously with facilitation, but nevertheless they are in charge. That would be considered appropriate for a university, but it's not even taken on board as a deliberate concept, and yet it's sort of happening, but it's happening because people are being let down. It's andragogy by mistake, without any care. Not only is it andragogy by mistake without care but it's school pedagogy, deliberately, without any care.

Gurpreet: Yes. Your care word is interesting to me. Lots of academics who I have worked with mix up care with student success and education. I have worked with some academics who I would consider to be very well meaning, decent, kind people, but they have delved too far into 'caring'. Which has not been educational. They haven't understood the difference between pastoral care and student success in education, and what their role is. As schoolteachers, they had a greater role for pastoral care because they were working with children. As university educators they're working with adult learners and it's the time then for pastoral care to be primarily dealt with by Student Support Services colleagues.

Academics, in my experience, can get too involved in issues they are not qualified to deal with. In the past I've had awful situations to unpick and resolve. These were problems which were actually created by academics. One horrible example was a female student with very difficult personal circumstances, and she was given some pastoral care advice by a male academic who was totally sexist. She was quite a young female student who didn't really understand what was going on, but she realized there was this overbearing, somewhat paternal, male academic advising her. She was quite rightly not comfortable with his advice and what he told her to do in that situation. I then had to unpick it and work with student services to sort out the issue. So 'care' is a problematic term in universities for me. I think it can be quite dangerous when some academics get involved in pastoral care issues.

Helen: He was trying to be the rescuer in a drama triangle where she is the victim. You had to unpick drama.

Gurpreet: I've had to talk to colleagues so many times and explain to them the drama triangle situation that they have got themselves into. It's a really important theory and especially important in universities. There can be some areas of universities that we work in that are toxic environments and there is bullying, in terms of the persecution aspect of the drama triangle. These areas of the university push people around the triangle positions, from bullying, to rescuing, to being the victim, and it can go round and round again. There are lots of benefits of universities that we haven't talked about, but the drama triangle is, I would say, pretty prevalent in universities. That is something that I didn't see in primary education when I worked there, although no doubt it exists. From my experience, I find it is a particular problem of higher education in England.

Helen: The book is attempting to offer students a way out of the university drama triangle and help them move into the winners' triangle. In that respect there is an emphasis on how a student – in universities which don't, in general, strike me as particularly wanting to improve how toxic they can be – can DIY themselves towards a sane response to that toxic potential. I fear it's not just that the university is a toxic environment due to a focus on competition but that this affects students badly when they enter the university, whether they know it or not. In other words students enter in innocently not knowing the air is polluted. If you go into a calm room with calm people, you feel calm or can calm down. You go into a drama-laden environment, it will 'touch' you somehow. Will this exacerbate existing or underlying anxieties or neuroses? Will students end up with mental health problems not because they have problems at the university but because the university is drawing them into being part of a toxic problem? Does university push people into forms of illness instead of wellness? There! The question is out.

It's a hard question, in so many ways. I'm curious what you think, given all your experience within a management role. You find yourself at the chalk-face of the inside of students' difficulties when they report these to survive the course, through getting an extension or whatever the conversation. There's criticism in this book about universities to the point where some universities might say students shouldn't read this book, it'll stop them wanting to enrol. That's not the point at all. The point is that university study can be a very useful thing to do and there is an education to be had at university level, but students must help themselves to avoid university drama, otherwise it's going to be a bad experience. I've heard of too many sad students and even student suicides. I don't want *anyone* killing themselves because they became a university student. *No one.* Paying to kill themselves through major incursion of fees? No. Universities must be safe. They must be careful how their environment operates at the level of personal emotional experience. So if the need is to be located in the winner's triangle, how do you think students can move into a position in that triangle: of acknowledging vulnerability, taking care of themselves and confidently speaking up for and looking for solutions?

Gurpreet: The mental health and well-being of students is a really important issue that you raise. We know there have been, unfortunately, far too many cases of suicide and accidental death in the last couple of years in English universities. I can only speak for England because that is where I am located and where I focus my attention. I think a positive development from one of those universities, which has spread a little bit, is that university students now, upon enrolment, can make the choice for the university to contact their parent-carer if they do become ill. But it's a very passive kind of agreement. Almost there, I think, for universities to protect themselves rather than to really support students. It has become a contract and tick-box. That is almost absolving universities of responsibility now. Universities are not at all primary care providers and I don't feel that we should be getting into that at all, as a university. But there is work that needs to be done by Student Support Services to proactively promote students' mental health and well-being. There needs to be far more signposting to students about all the support available.

In the past, I have had to chair final appeals from students who had buried their head in the sand rather than deal with their issues. Fortunately, they do come back and ask to rejoin the university. However, a common theme is that they have been mentally unwell in some way. They buried their head in the sand, did not seek support at the right time. Those are the good news stories. There are so many students I wouldn't have been able to see and get them back into university because they buried their head in the sand, they withdrew from the course and that was the end of their university education, which is such a shame. So there needs to be far more proactive support and signposting to students of what universities can do, but also reminding them of their GP support, for example. I'm not trying to give more responsibilities to universities. This applies especially when they are aged eighteen. Those students have just left the school environment and their family home. It's a really difficult period of transition for lots of them.

Helen: They've got that growing up thing but they've also got that learn to study at higher education level thing. These are two major steps up in terms of the responsibilities that they need to take for themselves. It all comes at once. Plus if I'm right – and I'm not saying I am, I'm curious – if a university is a troubled environment tipping people towards illness, then it doesn't help. A student who is already challenged by those two step-ups that we're talking about – and while some are having the thrill of their lives, others will be struggling – the answer is not to blame the student or stigmatize the student. That's a persecutory mode of drama. It would be to say to students, OK, these are your responsibilities: Can we help? That's like offering a winner's stance on a plate. Then if the student desires assistance, it's available, but there seems to be, you know, not enough clarity. Of a non-dramatic kind. What do you think?

Gurpreet: Yes and that goes back to my point about academics giving inaccurate advice. To say the least about the advice and example that I'm thinking of. The person has to give the right advice at the right time. It's our responsibility in universities to signpost students so that, for example, a young female student is not speaking to a male academic about a personal pastoral care matter, where actually he had no right and no expertise to advise her about the issues.

I think at the very, very early stages when students are even considering which university to go to, quite often now they will disclose a disability or a mental health issue to people at universities. What students need to realize, but unfortunately they don't, is that universities are businesses. They will promote to students their own university, encourage them to come to university, encourage them to pay hall of residence fees to live in that university environment, when actually for some students if they've got a really supportive family environment and family home, it would probably be much better for that student to go to a local university. Even if it isn't really their first choice, and it isn't as high a calibre a university as they really wanted to go to. Students need to go to the right university for them and that isn't always the right one academically. Universities across the country aren't going to turn away a student with mental health issues and say, 'Well, actually because of your problems and difficulties, by all means we will accept you here, but please consider a local university.' They won't say to a potential fee-paying student, 'It might be a more appropriate choice for you to remain in your family home.'

That doesn't happen because universities are businesses first and foremost and their first priority, as in any business, is institutional sustainability. They need to get as many students as possible into their institutions.

Helen: It's game playing based on reputational stakes. The reputation that they've got this many students, this much money, that they've got this percentage of people applying to them and they manage to reject that percentage, and therefore they are prestigious because it's a high reject rate because everyone wants to go there. All that. This is all game playing. But for students it isn't a game. It's their life. It's profoundly important for them and very personal.

These games are something about the university which has got nothing whatsoever to do with the acquisition and circulation of interesting ideas for the sake of the development of either the self or the world at large. It's something else entirely. Students seem to get caught in a web, a net. They become victims of this net.

Gurpreet: Yes. Sometimes they become victims of some of the academics. I've had lots of examples of students being weaponized by academic staff members to do untold damage to other academics. Students need to really remember that universities themselves have an agenda. They are a business. But also, quite often, *people* have an agenda too. The academics sometimes, if they're trying to weaponize them into complaining about someone, students need to remember that. The transactional analysis aspect is there. Academics quite often put themselves in a parent position and put the students into the child mode. University students go along with that because the parent, in this case the academic, is their assessor and they are in a position of power over them. So they get sucked into the transactional analysis dynamic of parent, child and also the drama triangle that we talked about earlier. Students get sucked into that and they don't know that they've been sucked into it because they are in an inferior position.

It's really troubling for me, the whole assessor issue, and the power issue. I feel that there is really a fundamental change that needs to happen in universities regarding assessment so that academic staff aren't in that power relationship with their students. If you think about in the English school system: we have a two-tiered assessment process. Teachers are teachers and yes, they assess their pupils formatively, but when it comes to summative assessments for GCSEs and A levels, those assignments go off to an independent exam board. OK, the exam boards are themselves businesses but they are at least totally independent of the school. Whereas in the university sector, we are the teacher, the tutor and the assessor. That is a conflict of interest. I find it very difficult to reconcile.

I consider that the reason why so many students get sucked into being used by academics is because the assessment system is unethical. Students know that if they speak out against a lecturer, it's highly likely that that will do them some damage in their assessment. Also in a small university, that's especially true because students can be identified far too easily. We say we have anonymous assignments, and anonymous marking, but it is, in fact, rhetoric. We can't have an ethical assessment process when it is a one-tier process. A university being the exam board isn't appropriate, so when academics are teachers, facilitators of learning, but they're also the assessor, that is a conflict of interest for them, and it's a conflict for students that puts students in a vulnerable position as a victim of the assessment procedure. It's no coincidence that every single year in the National Student Survey one of the worst responses is for the part 'students find assessment unfair'. Students every single year say they find assessment unfair.

Helen: What you're talking about is a situation that no one in their right mind would *pay* for. Yet students can incur long-term debt to pay for this.

Gurpreet: But there is no alternative. There is no university in the UK which undertakes assessment in a fair way. We have a veneer of fair assessment because we say that there's anonymized marking. We have external examiners to check the process is robust. But it is a veneer. Students struggle with it because they are used to a two-tier assessment process, where the teachers are not their assessors. It's the exam board that assesses and that is a healthy assessment process.

Helen: Universities ride – in terms of justifying a one-tier system for assessment – on the superstar-ness, the love of objectivity, the scientific brilliance of their academics, who are very far, they suggest, when providing only one tier of assessment, from any kind of corruption. Yet we know that you've got implicit bias, you've got stereotype threat, you've got all kinds of things that are circulating in the relational dynamics of a university. The least of which among these is definitely not power, because, as you rightly point out, power imbalance is a big problem. And yet universities are presenting themselves as beyond fault, and it's very important to them that the grades that they give out are seen as the right grades, the justifiable grades, the ones that mean something.

Gurpreet: What our assessment process does, and actually what our university system does, is perpetuate social injustice. We go around in circles, while universities are giving false promises of a transformative student experience, but it is often rhetoric of false promises. If only students were fully aware of how universities operate, their function, their benefits which are absolutely huge in broadening students' horizons, giving them the opportunities to do great placements and to meet different people on their courses. There are so many benefits to a university education. But students also need to educate themselves about the downsides of universities. We don't see any university websites which deviate away from saying they offer a transformative student-centred experience. But we know that is a show.

There are individual university academics who do offer a focus on students. That's wonderful and they are the really inspirational colleagues, but they are a minority. Students need to understand what they will get out of the university education and what they will need to do for themselves, because it's a flawed system, like most systems.

Helen: But in terms of the rhetoric and the publicizing PR spin and the reputational history – as I put it in the book, the fantasy, and others in this book have called it illusion or romanticism – the word that comes to mind as we talk is 'mirage'.

Gurpreet: Yes. So, universities present themselves in a certain way. Typically, in widening participation universities they present themselves as a university for everybody, whereas in a Russell Group university they present themselves like that with different shades, more emphasis on research clearly. But universities all present themselves in a very positive way because they are a business. They say what they need to say to attract students. No one is going to say anything that's warts and all. The website is their shop window and students need to study it well.

I really dislike that students have become customers in so many ways, but they are now paying for a university experience and so they do need to take a critical eye to the university that they choose, first of all. Also, throughout their studies. Because no university is perfect, they need to take a critical eye throughout their daily studies and their daily interactions with their academics and professional support staff. It's part of the microcosm of life. It isn't going to be a perfect environment. When students enter university they become a victim and inferior person because they feel that the power is elsewhere. They need to take that critical stance that they would take to something that was on social media, for example, or something one of their friends said. When it's in the university environment, students quite often take what is said to them as the absolute truth because it is said with authority, from a university, which has huge credibility. This is especially the case if it's a Russell Group ('top') university, but *most* universities speak in a very authoritative way. That's intimidating for students sometimes and they find that they can't challenge it.

Helen: It sort of floors me really. The whole thing. I know and you also know this. In fact, everybody that I've spoken to, despite what they've said at times as highly critical of universities themselves, knows that higher education level knowledge can transform a person. The book in various ways is talking about how you can get to that transformation and one of those ways is to be a critical witness to the environment. To not swallow it whole as the God-Given-Truth, because *it ain't.* It's a Dorian Gray scenario, really, isn't it?

Gurpreet: Yes. Absolutely. Yes. Students need to take that approach and have that idea of the mirror of Dorian Gray in front of them as they evaluate for themselves what is happening on a daily basis and make their own decisions, regarding what is right for them. It would be good really if students could work together more in collaborative ways, so that they are talking together. Not just, you know, as a social media 'rate my professor' approach. Those kinds of criticisms, which are very superficial, don't help. The students should get together as a strong community, in a positive way, not in a negative way. That just generates complaints, which I think are really unhealthy as part of the student culture. Students are encouraged to make formal complaints rather than resolve issues. Again that is really anti higher education because we need to have graduates who are critical thinkers and independent problem solvers.

For students to get together as a real community of learning where they work through issues and talk through issues in a safe learning environment, that could be a strategy for students to win, as you put it. To be in a healthy winner's triangle. But they certainly do need to take a critical eye to their studies as a part of their whole university experience and regard it in some ways as they would with other services they get involved with. I know that sounds very consumerist, and I don't want students ever to feel like consumers because they're not, they're there to expand their knowledge, broaden their horizons, learn in a whole range of ways: sometimes unintended learning outcomes. But that critical eye is really important throughout their studies.

Helen: Because otherwise they are not protecting themselves in what is a potentially, even likely – given everything that we've hinted at – rather violent environment. So the good news is if they take a critical eye and thereby protect themselves with a positive attitude and collaborate and cooperate with other students, they can have a good time, right? The facilities are there, the higher-level learning and ideas, discussion forums, possibilities for connection, these are all facilitated by the system that is the university.

It's brilliant at doing that. The thing that is not being protected because of this fantasy reputation bullshit is the emotional inner self. It's a lamb to the slaughter because you have to believe in the university, you have to give in to the university, you have to be the inferior partner in a power dynamic that's highly toxic. This is all like sacrificing yourself on an altar of what? Of long-term debt. So this book is saying *Enough!, Stop it!, Get real!* Given how arrogant universities are and how stubbornly conservative, the only person it seems to me capable of grabbing the power of *getting real* is the student themselves. Because they become, as you put it, educated through their critical eye and their questioning. They're not taking for granted the PR spin that is not just about the PR department of a particular university in a particular year with a particular campaign, it's a historical spin that is to do with aspiring to be a better person. So believing in the university as *unquestionably* beneficial goes very, very deep. It is a trap.

Gurpreet: Avoiding that trap takes a lot of determination from, in particular, young students. It takes criticality, it takes a lot of maturity, it takes a lot of hard work and also talent and determination to successfully complete your university studies but also to come out as a fully rounded person who has improved themselves in whatever way the student wanted to improve themselves there. But it very much comes down to the self. In England, we've now got the Office for Students, which purports to be an independent government body to protect students, but it isn't a body which protects students. It again is a government tool which really holds universities to account. In some ways it gives students additional layers of false promises because the Office for Students is holding universities to account about gaining graduate employment. Well, there are not enough graduate roles out there in the UK for all the graduates who can leave universities each year. They also hold universities to account on value for money. Well, you cannot really place value for money on a university education in that way. Again it gives students an extra layer of false promises. So the Office for Students purports to be an independent body to support students and that they're there for them. This false promising is what is happening in the English system.

Helen: At first I thought the solution to all this drama and hood-winking was you write, you write well, you're going to get the points, you're going to get the grades and you'll spin out as a winner in your black mortar board. That's no longer what I think *at all*. I think the student has to use the university, *just* as they are being used. Writing well is the way to the grades but the problem of how to play is much bigger, much deeper, much more political than merely about academic performance.

Gurpreet: Yes. They need to use the university as a service. They have to have that almost consumer mentality, but with positivity. To get what they need out of the university education that they are paying for in so many ways. They have to know that universities are a business. But they shouldn't accept that universities are being *led* like businesses. They should be business-like, but they shouldn't tolerate that universities are being led like businesses. Because then that enables students to be treated badly. I've had examples of students being treated in sexist ways, in racist ways, so many examples of poor treatment. If students did take that critical, mature eye to their studies, they could really protect themselves.

I don't think students at the moment are in a good place when they're trying to challenge universities, because they come off worse. I would not advocate that they tried to challenge universities because that goes to the fundamental root of the university system, which isn't going to change anytime soon. They need to protect themselves and get from the universities, as you say, what they need. To take that approach is a very pragmatic approach, but it's also a principled pragmatic approach.

Helen: This profile of the student protecting themselves, using the university, being realistic and being critical, is going to help the student play and win the game of being at university. How?

Gurpreet: Because they have identified their needs. They graduate with whatever they wanted to happen for them. For some students that will be a graduate-level job. For some students it will be something else. It will have been horizons broadened, it will have been a life-changing experience in meeting new people and really transforming their personal lives. So it's very individual. It would be good for students to be able to identify for themselves what they need to get out of their university education. Then they can prioritize those aspects which matter to them most, so that then it is a successful and transformative experience in whatever way they needed it to be.

Lots of students and their families go without. I don't just mean financially but also there are emotional costs. Students go without so much to pay for a university education, in whatever way or means they need to do so. They have *got* to come out with whatever they need for them. They need to make it a really good experience. The sacrifices of a university education, particularly for poorer families, are immense.

It really pains me that we have so many students in our universities who are going without and yet we have got a university system and so many academics, quite often, staffing universities who put themselves first, rather than the students first. That is the absolute priority for me. Our students often are going without for this experience. We have got to make it a better experience for them, because they only get one chance at it.

Helen: But by better experience, do you mean a less one-sided egotistical experience? In that the university is egotistical and many academics are egotistical. For students, now it's about time they started to say, '*I am going to transform myself* and the university is what I'm paying to enable me to do that. And, by the way, university, by the way, academics, you might be egotistical, but you haven't seen any ego yet, because I've just arrived, this ego here, the one that's paying.' By that I don't mean to suggest that some arse of a student walks into the university and causes chaos. Rather that the student empowers themselves through a positive, fruitful, beneficial use of their own ego to cope with and navigate university territory. Students have voice if they'd only feel they can use it and they deserve for that voice to be heard and respected.

Gurpreet: Absolutely. In that position we would have a truly student-centred experience where at the moment we have quite often a self-centred university experience, based on the egos of academics and the universities as institutions and as businesses. But students have got to work themselves to make that possible for them. Wouldn't it be wonderful if we had a university ethos where – if you think about NASA everybody apparently is saying whatever their role, the cleaner said: 'I am helping to put a man (or woman!) on the moon.' Wouldn't it be great if we had universities where you ask the cleaner or the Vice Chancellor in the university and a whole range of different people what they did and they all said, 'I'm helping to transform students' lives.' Wouldn't that be brilliant! But there are too many egos in the university to allow that to happen. When we do have a university ethos where everybody could say that and it was all about the students, then we would have a truly student-centred experience.

Helen: While we are waiting and in absence of such an ethos, this book suggests to students in no uncertain terms, that they take matters *into their own hands*. They need to be the ones who say, 'I am serving students.'

Gurpreet: Yes. I really like the term 'serving' as well, Helen, because servant leadership and serving students is what *we* should be doing, rather than being self-serving. That would be a truly student-centred experience if we were serving our students and if everybody remembered we were serving the academic function *for* the students.

Helen: Well, thereby we end, but at the same time you and I both know that we're talking in dreamland there. This revolution of the student being served is only going to happen if students do it.

Gurpreet: I do feel hopeful. When you think about climate change and different campaigns that have happened over the last few years, I feel really positive about the younger generation and that they will not accept some of the inappropriate behaviours and bias and discrimination that my generation has faced. I do feel really positive. Coming back to where I started, I still feel, despite everything I said, I still feel very optimistic about university education. It can be a truly transformative experience if students really understand and make themselves aware of what they are getting themselves into and how they're going to work through the process for themselves. So I feel very idealistic, despite my pessimism about some of the real flaws of the university system. The younger generation – seeing how they are behaving and taking that more critical eye with climate change – there is absolutely no reason why they can't do that with higher education. I think there is a lot of hope for the future with the next generation that's coming through.

A Serious Game But Not That Serious

Studying at university is a game. As John Cage says, 'I think much in our society becomes endurable if it's realized that it's a game; and not more serious than that' (John Cage speaking in Kostelanetz 2003: 283). This holds for the university. Whatever is right or wrong about higher education environments perhaps we can enjoy these spaces for all their benefits if we don't take them quite so seriously?

However, people getting hurt is serious. People need to stand up for how the university affects students as an environment when that affect may be harmful, but we need to know more: 'Research examining risks and buffers to mental health in students is needed to try and untangle *the various effects of university life* on student mental health' (Cooke et al. 2004: 63, emphasis added). We do know you, as a student, matter more than the university.

'Students' lives are becoming increasingly pressurised' (Cooke et al. 2006: 505). Why? If we are to understand a shocking situation of universities being possibly *dangerous* for one's health we need research that can 'incorporate a baseline prior to students' arrival at university' (Cooke et al. 2006: 506). If we don't yet know how to understand the extent of the effect of a university on a person, we need to know, at least, how to mitigate negativity and safeguard against it. There is an effect. There is a need to safeguard. A lack of a baseline for judging the impact on people of university cultures and management mechanisms means we do not know enough about how the university might need to be *responsible* for the impact and effects it has on the people who enter in. Not just responsible for their certificates but also for personal and interpersonal outcomes attributable to the university as activity, environment and business. The university as an experience might need to take account of the vulnerability it *causes*. Hall says universities 'depend upon anxiety as a dynamic force' and they cause 'ill-being, as individuals and departments compete for resources' (see Hall 2021, chapter 2). I agree.

The university as an idea and as a reality charges a lot of money to join in its game. Yet, itself, it pays too little heed to its own culpability in this respect of causing 'ill-being', implying students are at fault or fallible: 'This is not a case of [university] employers admitting that structural problems are the source of employees' distress. On the contrary, both students and staff have been accused of lacking resilience' (Morrish 2019: 39). So it's a tough game? They don't write that up in the brochures nor the employment contracts. They could have a page (preferably front page) or a clause that reads something like this: 'If you join this space you need to take responsibility for yourself, because we don't care.'

Unfortunately and unnecessarily the university as concept, and far too often as practice, has a harsh, unyielding and undemocratic face. I frame this much like the school as institution has historically blamed school students and families for truancy, bad behaviour, failings and ill-being, when, in fact, the school was – and is – significantly the culpable and responsible (irresponsible) harming party all along (Pilkington and Piersel 1991; Carlen et al. 1992; Yoneyama 1999, 2000; Yoneyama and Naito 2003; Harber 2004, 2008, 2009a). Schools harm people. Universities harm people.

I feel the stress and strains of the inhumanity of universities as personal experience are their shame. It should never be our shame for we are not the responsible party for the distress. Their *lack* of responsibility taken is why we need, after waiting in vain for them to shape up, to bring the matter of responsibility into our own hands and self-educate, self-manage and self-protect.

Universities ought to manage themselves both less and better: less managerialism and more awareness of how people need to experience the acquisition and development of knowledge kindly, through filters of compassion, not condescension. We can dodge what universities have become by not becoming tainted with their drama. That does involve working on ourselves to have a robust, solid sense of self or else we are likely to be sucked in and negatively affected. Compassless we lose ourselves there. Enjoying a university is sometimes hard work, sometimes the easiest and most glorious experience of joy. They are contradictory places. Contradiction is not an excuse for danger.

One way forward is for them to stop lying and develop a more nuanced picture of how they promise. It is simply not good enough that universities actively avoid responsibility to tell the truth: '[it was] noted how prospectuses resembled a cross between a teen magazine and a tourist brochure . . . . Everyone is smiling. There is never any stress, disappointment or grinding hard work on our lovely campus!' (Connell 2019: 131). Universities need to have a warning sign on the front door I'm afraid, not a welcome mat.

Questions, then, at the heart of this book, in light of some doubts about the university project as personally, morally, psychologically and socially good, are: Do we really need or want to go to university? What is the existential story to be told by the university graduate or staff member of their time at university? Why pay all that money or endure serious sacrifices to encounter harm? Why pay all that money or endure those sacrifices at all? Is there another way to gain knowledge and credentials? The point of such questions is to ensure that no one feels pressurized to copy the spirit of brochure lies. We need to be enabled to live more authentically in relation to the idea of the university through such questioning.

For a higher *level* of education and scholarship activity, university is not the only system we have. You can get, be and become educated or educate by many pathways. Some of them are fiscally relatively free to follow or offer to others teaching without a student being charged a high university profit margin. You can follow an academic career outside of universities. These pathways are possibly longer and more difficult for being outside of institutional supports but being without the university as matrix might be more collegiate, possibly more open, more creative, real fun and less dramatic (Neary and Winn 2016; Meyerhoff 2019). It's hard to generalize. It's hard to know which pathway would be best for any given individual: for you. A self-designed pathway or a course? Relative game-less freedom to be or a tension-characterized game in a matrix with extensive facilities? What is clear is that for other ways to function people need to robustly self-educate and profoundly DIY their pathway whether inside the university or outside its frame. This is the way forward for education because education as institutional has let so many of us *personally* down so often and so fundamentally. From childhood onwards. As an adult relationship, universities do not relate well enough to *people* for you to trust their pathway will serve and care for you. I'm suggesting you self-educate because universities are selfish.

If higher education knowledge is nowadays out there via the internet to reach towards at a click, then every click is positive self-centred self-care. Most academics share their work as freely as they can. Literature to study with is within reach without paying. There are dedicated websites where academics post their academic work outside of publisher's paywalls. If you look at (after creating for yourself an access profile) researchgate.net, unpaywall.org, VIVO, Mendeley, Epernicus, academia.edu or search on the internet for 'how to get around academia paywall' you'll see what I mean: you can get free access to academic research articles. Although these largely demand some sign of a university-level affiliation there is possible access via describing yourself as an 'independent scholar', as I do. A movement for open access – the absence of paywalls to access academic research – is in motion and 'growing up' (Joseph 2013). Universities put course reading lists online. Nowadays learnt skills, informative presentations and MOOC (massive open online course) sites like coursera.org, edX.org, futurelearn .com, udacity.com, domestika.org, ted.com, youtube.com and many others offer gateways to different kinds and levels of learning at small, if any cost. More information and rationale about a 'DIY' university education is found in a variety of exciting literature (see, e.g. Kamenetz 2010; Roksa 2011; Neary and Winn 2016; Caplan 2018; Meyerhoff 2019). Local organized 'non' universities, with study happening at university level, are being created, offering a 'vision of an alternative, cooperative, higher education, dedicated to the public good' (Noble and Ross 2019: vi). This wide variety of voices and approaches begins to democratize the idea of gaining and mastering knowledge. It points towards non-university-based higher-level self-education.

Yet there is a caveat to note and deal with carefully. What is hard to gain this way is the culture of discernment universities protect. This aspect is born of generations of often appropriate snobbery about quality, based on expertise, peer review factors where academic colleagues 'quality check' each other's work. In a university (or with educated scholarly others) you encounter this atmosphere of discernment and it is an education in itself. Such peer reviewing is not a perfect system and clearly it is sometimes too brusque or thoughtless. Sometimes it is plain wrong. Also, thought thus validated can be biased towards those groups with most power. But this community of peers – most often found through university connection – is useful and offers improvements in what is shared, either for public view or private discussions. The art of peer review and of accepting feedback is a serious one, worth your trouble. Published research has usually gone through a 'discernment' process already and the university system does support this in a profound way. The essence of the matter for you, wherever you learn, is: triangulate your knowledge. Take more than one opinion and compare perspectives. Read more than one perspective. Enjoy more than one perspective. Need a multitude of ideas to be right. Don't believe everything you read. Critique when you discover. Avoid and learn to recognize fakery. Aim for authentic knowledge, which is not quite as obvious, or as easy, as it sounds.

Despite my concerns and my own personal choice to live, study and pursue knowledge outside a university matrix, I enjoyed and enjoy the university. As a space for studying, either as a student or as a teacher, it is a great educational utility. I've met such wonderful people there. I've had such a laugh there at times. You will, or you can too. At a university you learn how to think among practised thinkers, you interact with their fabulous minds, you learn how to write among other writers (of the academic genre) and gain feedback from experts in such writing. You have unfettered access to so much wonderful literature as well as close proximity to fellow curious seekers of new thoughts and ways to think who all, similarly to you, have dedicated time to that activity in order to discover knowledge in your discipline. It's a great package of mental stimulation and excitement. But it is expensive and a clearly troubled, insecure environment. The good with the bad needs careful consideration. Context for this that we absolutely have to have now with the problems of climate change is that *we are embedded* in our world with care, not floating above it, uncaringly, selfishly striving to be number one. If universities perpetuate and perpetrate the idea that we need to be number one and that to be this they are the answer, then they are culpably involved in the limiting destruction of required diversity of people, pathways to knowledge and new ways of being and thinking. We need flourishing *diversity*, not cookie cutting, if our planet is to survive.

We are very few of us ready for university when we stand at the gates. It ought to be a hard and well-thought-out decision to give up all the other possible lives we could lead to attend a university space for *that* kind of learning. While I have thoroughly enjoyed and appreciated the opportunity for my research work, which itself would not have been possible without my fraught, failed and upsetting undergraduate time and its consequent just-achieved certificate, I could have done it differently and had similar joy elsewhere, by other means. Certainly gaining a first degree was for me a key move to open doors towards higher salary careers, but money isn't everything. The system that demands university certification needs challenging. Our purpose in life is unlikely to be the making of money because money does not contribute, it takes. If university is only a gateway to money then lots of students are walking in the wrong direction if they seek purpose.

It is not hard to imagine that thinking for yourself and carefully about what higher education route you decide to take is important work of the self – especially given the potential for debt some pathways involve, which is really serious as long-term outcome (Cooke et al. 2004; Dwyer et al. 2011). *Blindly* following the seemingly only given path of university entrance is an expensive lack of effort. Becoming better educated *does not rely* on a university. Education and a degree are two distinct things with the first being important in and of itself. The better educated we are, the more we know; the more nuanced and complex we see the world as, the better our opinions, actions, decisions and treatment of others. Also, possibly, our understanding of self improves with education, which is a really important goal. Feel free not to go to university. We don't need a system to tell us we are OK.

The university as institution needs to shift paradigm. Will it? Don't hold your breath. Do see rule 4! ☺. Universities have lost touch with humility and with reality. Reality is that people really, really matter. How they are treated, how they get to treat each other, what they experience and what they learn about life and living in university spaces are worthy of better attention by universities, for inter-relational details are the formation of thinking. Perhaps this serious-non-serious game is toughening us up for the outside world and doing us a favour? They used to say that about bullying in schools. Then they realized that, actually, bullying is not formative at all. It is terribly harmful to people through the life course and entirely avoidable if the institution of the school addresses the problems within its own walls that are allowing bullying to occur. As ever, care and compassion for self and the other matter so very much. University leaders cannot fail us.

Having devised a clear understanding of the long-term impacts through the life course, pros and cons, of attending university, go for it, or not. Your decision, informed and clearly your own, is the decision of a winner. However you play their game, if you play, be a winner because you care for yourself with kindness and compassion. Becoming educated in some way at a higher education *level*, for some purpose of yours, is a serious, brilliant game. Believe in higher education. Good luck!

Notes

Introducing the Game We Play

1 Throughout this book reference to the term 'violent' or 'violence' in connection with educational environments intends forms of symbolic violence, interpersonal drama as a terror, ego as a violence against equality and other such interactional uses. It rarely would include the idea of physical violence, although there is awareness that just as with any heavily populated environment, physical violence can and does occur in 'tense' environments, albeit, hopefully, rarely.

2 Some disciplines do not see writing as their main piece of 'sports equipment'. Chemists might do chemical substance experiments as a primary activity? Those doing a dance degree would dance more than write? An aviation degree would require lots of flying? Art degree students might sculpt, paint or take photographs? Please see the word and focus in this book on *writing* as a way to talk about disciplinary performances using peer review (this hopefully might somehow involve also fellow students, as well as the usual take on who decides a mark: academic staff). Writing here then includes, as idea, having course work of *whatever kind* submitted and marked according to a quality control guide document (itself a contestable manner of understanding the state of someone's knowledge). I apologize to those disciplinary students reading this who might feel alienated by the strong use of writing, if this isn't their mode of working. The emphasis on writing is largely due to the discipline I come from (social sciences). Also, it is because it is impossible to coherently include all manner and forms of assessment by their actual names and, honestly, having not done all degrees available I'm not sure how not-writing-based disciplines do their assessments. If writing is not your main tool please do mentally transpose your own subject's assessment modes where this is relevant.

Chapter 1

1 I am well aware that the story I present and elucidate in this conversation with Eli seems quite dramatic at times. Also other conversations in this book might seem sometimes dramatic. All books are, after all, *stories* being told; even non-fiction, academic texts. I hope this book seeks a situation of presenting a need for accountability and of taking responsibility on the part of all parties. If I have in any way failed in that task, in any degree, that is my responsibility.

This is not me owning up to weakness or washing my hands. It is to frame everything here as an inherent part of the winners' triangle where none are wholly innocent nor wholly blameless and moving forwards is only found in and with cooperation and calm collaboration. This might not be dramatically sexy as a footnote, but it is sane and healthily helpful, recognizing that there is no black and white, no generalizations that hold as such, even when we lament a state of affairs. We are all entitled to our views and in a non-dramatic scenario no view, if responsibility is held, is persecutory.

Chapter 4

1 Use of the term 'examination' or 'examiner' in this conversation includes the idea of formative marked essays and feedback as well as summative end of semester or year exams, under exam conditions.

Chapter 7

1 See conversation with Eli Meyerhoff in this book.

References

Ang, I. (1996), *Watching Dallas: Soap Opera and the Melodramatic Imagination*, London: Routledge.

Anonymous (2021), 'Academic Freedom Must Include the Right to Criticise Employers', *Times Higher Education*. https://www.timeshighereducation.com/blog/academic-freedom-must-include-right-criticise-employers.

Belenky, M., B. Clinchy, N. Goldberger and J. Tarule (1997), *Women's Ways of Knowing: The Development of Self, Voice, and Mind*, 10th Anniversary edn., New York: Basic Books.

Biggs, J. and C. Tang (2011), *Teaching for Quality Learning at University*, Maidenhead, UK: SRHE/McGraw Hill.

Bingham, C. (2008), *Authority is Relational*, Albany: State University of New York Press.

Bok, D. (2004), *Universities in the Marketplace: The Commercilaization of Higher Education*, Princeton: Princeton University Press.

Bolaño, R. (2004), *2666*, Barcelona: Vintage Español.

Bousquet, M. (2008), *How the University Works: Higher Education and the Low-Wage Nation*, New York: New York University Press.

Bowles, S. and H. Gintis (1976), *Schooling in Capitalist America*, London: Routledge and Kegan Paul.

Brennan, J. and P. W. Magness (2019), *Cracks in the Ivory Tower: The Moral Mess of Higher Education*, New York: Oxford University Press.

Cahalan, M. (2013), *Widening Participation in Higher Education in the United States of America*, Leicester: HEFCE.

Caplan, B. (2018), *The Case Against Education: Why the Education System is a Waste of Time and Money*, Princeton: Princeton University Press.

Carlen, P., D. Gleeson and J. Wardhaugh (1992), *Truancy: The Politics of Compulsory Schooling*, Buckingham: Open University Press.

Chatterjee, P. and S. Maira, eds (2014), *The Imperial University: Academic Repression and Scholarly Dissent*, Minneapolis: The University of Minnesota.

Choy, A. (1990), 'The Winner's Triangle', *Transactional Analysis Journal*, 20 (1): 40–6.

Collini, S. (2017), *Speaking of Universities*, London: Verso.

Connell, R. (2019), *The Good University: What Universities Actually Do and Why It's Time for Radical Change*, London: Zed Books.

Cooke, R., M. Barkham, K. Audin and M. Bradley (2004), 'Student Debt and Its Relation to Student Mental Health', *Journal of Further and Higher Education*, 28 (1): 53–66.

Cooke, R., B. M. Bewick, M. Barkham, M. Bradley and K. Audin (2006), 'Measuring, Monitoring and Managing the Psychological Well-Being of First

Year University Students', *British Journal of Guidance & Counselling*, 34 (4): 505–17.

Coughlan, S. (2015, 30 September), 'Rising Numbers of Stressed Students Seek Help', *BBC*. Available online: http://www.bbc.co.uk/news/education-34354405 (accessed 15 January 2015).

Craig, R. (2018), 'America's Colleges and Universities are Just Like "Fantasy Island"', Available online: https://www.forbes.com/sites/ryancraig/2018/07/26/americas-colleges-and-universities-are-just-like-fantasy-island/?sh=aa22b44450ba (accessed 20 December 2020).

Cron, L. (2012), *Wired for Story: The Writer's Guide to Using Brain Science to Hook Readers from the Very First Sentence*, New York: Ten Speed Press.

Culver, R. (2021), 'Intro to The Survive/Thrive Spiral (Video)', Available online: http://calmheart.co.uk/spiralvideo/.

Devlin, M. (7 March 2021), 'No Change at the Top for University Leaders as Men Outnumber Women 3 to 1', *The Conversation*. https://theconversation.com/no-change-at-the-top-for-university-leaders-as-men-outnumber-women-3-to-1-154556.

Dwyer, R. E., L. McCloud and R. Hodson (2011), 'Youth Debt, Mastery, and Self-Esteem: Class-Stratified Effects of Indebtedness on Self-Concept', *Social Science Research*, 40 (3): 727–41.

Earley, J. (2009), *Self-Therapy: A Step-By-Step Guide to Creating Wholeness and Healing Your Inner Child Using IFS, A New, Cutting-Edge Psychotherapy*, Larkspur: Pattern System Books.

Ellen, B. (2017), 'Universities Now Sell Themselves – Just Like Shampoo', *The Guardian*.

Ergül, H. and S. Coşar, eds (2017), *Universities in the Neoliberal Era: Academic Cultures and Critical Perspectives*, London: Palgrave.

Erricker, C. and J. Erricker, eds (2001), *Meditation in Schools: Calmer Classrooms*, London: Continuum.

Fleming, P. (2021), *Dark Academia: How Universities Die*, London: Pluto Press.

Flint, K. J. and N. Peim (2012), *Rethinking the Education Improvement Agenda: A Critical Philosophical Approach*, London: Continuum.

Foucault, M. (1977), *Discipline and Punish*, London: Penguin.

Foucault, M. (1980), *Power/Knowledge – Selected Interviews and Other Writings 1972–1977*, New York: Pantheon Books.

Foucault, M. (2001), *Fearless Speech*, Los Angeles: Semiotext.

Gatto, J. T. (1992), *Dumbing Us Down: The Hidden Curriculum of Compulsory Schooling*, Gabriola Island: New Society Publishers.

Geoghegan, M. (2021), 'The Real Threat to Free Speech on Campus is the NDA', *Times Higher Education*. https://www.timeshighereducation.com/blog/real-threat-free-speech-campus-nda.

Gerlock, J. (2012), 'Sense of Community Online: Self-regulated Learning and Avoiding the Drama Triangle', Master of Counselling, University of Lethbridge.

Gibbs, P. and A. Peterson, eds (2019), *Higher Education and Hope Institutional, Pedagogical and Personal Possibilities*, London: Palgrave.

Goodman, P. (1971), *Compulsory Miseducation*, London: Penguin.

Goodsman, D. (1992), 'Summerhill: Theory and Practice', Unpublished PhD thesis, University of East Anglia, Norwich.

Svensson, g. and G. Wood (2007), 'Are University Students Really Customers? When Illusion May Lead to Delusion for All!', *International Journal of*

Educational Management, 21 (1): 17–28. https://doi.org/10.1108/09513540710716795.

Gorczynski, P. (2018), 'More Academics and Students Have Mental Health Problems than Ever Before', Available online: https://theconversation.com/more-academics-and-students-have-mental-health-problems-than-ever-before-90339.

Gray, L.-A. (2019), *Educational Trauma: Examples From Testing to the School-to-Prison Pipeline*, Cham, Switzerland: Palgrave Macmillan.

Greenberg, D. and M. Sadofsky (1992), *Legacy of Trust; Life After the Sudbury Valley School Experience*, Framingham: Sudbury Valley School Press.

Guinier, L. (2015), *The Tyranny of the Meritocracy: Democratizing Higher Education in America*, Boston: Beacon Press.

Gutiérrez y Muhs, G., Y. Flores Niemann, C. G. González and A. P. Harris, eds (2012), *Presumed Incompetent: The Intersections of Race and Class for Women in Academia*, Boulder: University Press of Colorado.

Hall, R. (2014), 'On the University as Anxiety Machine', Available online: http://www.richard-hall.org/2014/03/19/on-the-university-as-anxiety-machine/.

Hall, R. (2021), *The Hopeless University: Intellectual Work at the End of the End of History*, Leicester: Mayfly Books.

Hall, R. and K. Bowles (2016), 'Re-engineering Higher Education: The Subsumption of Academic Labour and the Exploitation of Anxiety', *Workplace: A Journal for Academic Labor*, 28: 30–47.

Haralambos, M. and M. Holborn (2014), *Sociology: Themes and Perspectives*, 8th edn., London: Collins.

Harber, C. (2004), *Schooling as Violence: How Schools Harm Pupils and Societies*, London: Routledge Falmer.

Harber, C. (2008), 'Perpetrating Disaffection: Schooling as an International Problem', *Educational Studies*, 34 (5): 457–67.

Harber, C. (2009a), *Toxic Schooling: How Schools Became Worse*, Nottingham: Educational Heretics Press.

Havergal, C. (2019), 'Stop Gagging Harassment Victims, Minister to Tell UK Universities', *Times Higher Education*. https://www.timeshighereducation.com/news/stop-gagging-harassment-victims-minister-tell-uk-universities.

Huppert, F. A. and D. M. Johnson (2010), 'A Controlled Trial of Mindfulness Training in Schools: The Importance of Practice for an Impact on Well-Being', *Journal of Positive Psychology*, 5 (4): 264–74.

James, M. and D. Jongeward (1971), *Born to Win: Transactional Analysis with Gestalt Experiments*, Cambridge: Da Capo Press.

Joseph, H. (2013), 'The Open Access Movement Grows Up: Taking Stock of a Revolution', *Plos Biology*, 11 (10): 1–3.

Kabat-Zinn, J. (2005), *Coming to Our Senses: Healing and the World Through Mindfulness*, New York: Hyperion.

Kamenetz, A. (2010), *DIY U: Edupunks, Edupreneurs, and the Coming Transformation of Higher Education*, White River Junction: Chelsea Green Publishing.

Karpman, S. (2014), *A Game Free Life. The Definitive Book on the Drama Triangle and Compassion Triangle by the Originator and Author. The New Transactional Analysis of Intimacy, Openness, and Happiness*, San Francisco: Drama Triangle Publications.

Karpman, S. B. (1968), 'Fairy Tales and Script Drama Analysis', *Transactional Analysis Bulletin*, 7 (26): 39–43.

Karpman, S. B. (2007), 'The New Drama Triangles', *USATAA/ITAA Conference*, San Francisco.

Kauffman, D. R. and F. J. Perry (1989), 'Institutionalized Sexism in Universities: The Case of Geographically Bound Academic Women', *NWSA Journal*, 1 (4): 644–59.

Kierkegaard, S. (1985), *Fear and Trembling*, London: Penguin.

Kostelanetz, R. (2003), *Conversing with Cage*, New York: Routledge.

Labaree, D. F. (2017), *A Perfect Mess: The Unlikely Ascendancy of American Higher Education*, Chicago: The University of Chicago Press.

Lees, H. E. (2011), 'The Gateless Gate of Home Education Discovery: What Happens to the Self of Adults Upon Discovery of the Possibility and Possibilities of an Educational Alternative?', PhD, University of Birmingham. Available online: http://etheses.bham.ac.uk/1570/.

Lees, H. E. (2012), *Silence in Schools*, London: Trentham Books.

Lees, H. E. (2013a), 'Is the Idea of Compulsory Schooling Ridiculous?', in M. Papastephanou (ed.), *Philosophical Perspectives on Compulsory Education*, 143–56. Dortrecht: Springer.

Lees, H. E. (2013b), 'Solitude, Silence, Serenity and Pausing: The Missing Philosophical Story of Education', in *Philosophy of Education Society of Great Britain Conference 2013*, Oxford.

Lees, H. E. (2014), *Education Without Schools: Discovering Alternatives*, Bristol: Policy Press.

Lees, H. E. (2015), '"I Have No Idea What I'm Talking About"—Education (Studies) as Mutilation of Self', *British Educational Research Association Conference*. Belfast.

Lees, H. E. and L. C. Gualda (trans.) (2018), 'Hanging Around, Pottering About, Chilling Out: Lessons on Silence and Well-Being from Summerhill School. Andando pelo ambiente, passeando, relaxando: lições sobre silêncio e bem-estar da Summerhill School', *Revista Hipótese* 4(1), 194–214. Retrieved from https://revistahipotese.emnuvens.com.br/revista/article/view/310.

Lees, H. E. and E. Meyerhoff (2020), 'Book Reviews: An Exchange - Beyond Education: Radical Studying for Another World by Eli Meyerhoff- An Exchange as a Review Between Helen E. Lees and Author of Beyond Education, Eli Meyerhoff', *Other Education*, 9 (2): 113–20.

Lees, H. E. and N. Noddings, eds (2016), *The Palgrave International Handbook of Alternative Education*, London: Palgrave.

LeViness, P., K. Gorman, L. Braun, L. Koenig and C. Bershad (2019), 'The Association for University and College Counseling Center Directors Annual Survey: 2019', Reporting period: 1 July 2018 through 30 June 2019. Available online: https://www.aucccd.org/assets/documents/Survey/2019%20AUCCCD%20Survey-2020-05-31-PUBLIC.pdf: AUCCCD.

Lew, B, J. Huen, P. Yu, L. Yuan, D. F. Wang, F. Ping, M. Abu Talib, D. Lester and C. X. Jia (2019), 'Associations Between Depression, Anxiety, Stress, Hopelessness, Subjective Well-Being, Coping Styles and Suicide in Chinese University Students', *PLoS One*, 1 (7): 1.

Lloyd, G. (1984), *The Man of Reason: 'Male' and 'Female' in Western Philosophy*, London: Routledge.

Lyotard, J.-F. (1984), *The Postmodern Condition: A Report on Knowledge*, Manchester: Manchester University Press.

Lyotard, J.-F. (1985), *Just Gaming*, Minneapolis: University of Minnesota Press.

Mayo, N. (2019), 'University Staff "At Breaking Point" as Counselling Demand Soars. Hepi Report Ties Increase to Mounting Workloads and Performance Management', *Times Higher Education Supplement*, London. https://www.timeshighereducation.com/news/university-staff-breaking-point-counselling-demand-soars.

McCallam, D. (2020), 'The University Now: A Provocation in Five Readings', *Other Education*, 9 (2): 62–74.

McCloud, T. and D. Bann (2019), 'Financial Stress and Mental Health Among Higher Education Students in the UK Up To 2018: Rapid Review of Evidence', *Journal of Epidemiol Community Health*, 0: 1–8.

McKimm, J. and K. Forrest (2010), 'Using Transactional Analysis to Improve Clinical and Educational Supervision: The Drama and Winner's Triangles', *Postgraduate Medical Journal*, 86: 261–5.

Mettler, S. (2014), *Degrees of Inequality: How the Politics of Higher Education Sabotaged the American Dream*. New York: Basic Books.

Meyerhoff, E. (2019), *Beyond Education: Radical Studying for Another World*, Minnesota: Minnesota University Press.

Mistler, B. J., D. R. Reetz, B. Krylowicz and V. Barr (2012), 'The Association for University and College Counseling Center Directors Annual Survey', Reporting period: 1 September 2011 through 31 August 2012. Available online: http://files.cmcglobal.com/Monograph_2012_AUCCCD_Public.pdf: AUCCCD.

Morrish, L. (2017), 'Why the Audit Culture Made Me Quit', *Times Higher Education*, London. https://www.timeshighereducation.com/features/why-audit-culture-made-me-quit.

Morrish, L. (2019), *Pressure Vessels: The Epidemic of Poor Mental Health Among Higher Education Staff*, Oxford: HEPI.

Neary, M. (2016), 'Student as Producer: The Struggle for the Idea of the University', *Other Education*, 5 (1): 89–94.

Neary, M. and J. Winn (2016), 'Beyond Public and Private: A Framework for Co-operative Higher Education', *Co-operative Education Conference*, 21–22nd April, Manchester.

Nelson, C. (1997), 'Superstars', *Academe*, 83 (1): 38–43.

Nelson, C. and S. Watts (1999), *Academic Keywords: A Devil's Dictionary For Higher Education*, New York: Routledge.

Nhat Hanh, T. (1990), *Breathe! You are Alive; Sutra on the Full Awareness of Breathing*, London: Rider.

Noble, M. and C. Ross, eds (2019), *Reclaiming the University for the Public Good: Experiments and Futures in Co-operative Higher Education*, Cham, Switzerland: Palgrave MacMillan.

O'Sullivan, M. (2016), *Academic Barbarism, Universities and Inequality*, Basingstoke: Palgrave MacMillan.

Ollin, R. (2008), 'Silent Pedagogy and Rethinking Classroom Practice: Structuring Teaching Through Silence Rather Than Talk', *Cambridge Journal of Education*, 38 (2): 265–80.

Orr, D. (2002), 'The Uses of Mindfulness in Anti-Oppressive Pedagogies: Philosophy and Praxis', *Canadian Journal of Education*, 27 (4): 477–90.

Orr, D. (2012), 'Thinking Outside the Academic Box: An Introduction to Mindfulness Meditation for Education', *Other Education*, 1 (1): 79–91.

Parr, C. (2014), 'Attempts to "Gag and Silence" Academics Re Commonplace', *Times Higher Education*. https://www.timeshighereducation.com/news/attempts-to-gag-and-silence-academics-are-commonplace/2015692.article.

Patten, K. (1997), 'Teaching "Discovering Silence"', in A. Jaworski (ed.), *Silence: Interdisciplinary Perspectives*, 369–78, Berlin and New York: Mouton de Gruyter.

Peim, N. (2012), 'The Big Other: An Offer You Can't Refuse – Or Accept, in Some Cases. Education as Onto-Theological Principle (Empire): An Anti-Manifesto', *Other Education*, 1 (1): 226–38.

Peim, N. and K. J. Flint (2009), 'Testing Times: Questions Concerning Assessment for School Improvement', *Educational Philosophy and Theory*, 41 (3): 342–61.

Peters, M. A. (2019), 'Manifesto for the Postcolonial University', *Educational Philosophy and Theory*, 51 (2): 142–8.

Pilkington, C. L. and W. C. Piersel (1991), 'School Phobia – A Critical Analysis of the Separation Anxiety Theory and an Alternative Conceptualization', *Psychology in the Schools*, 28 (4): 290–303.

Rogers, I. H. (2012), *The Black Campus Movement: Black Students and the Racial Reconstitution of Higher Education, 1965–1972*, New York: Palgrave MacMillan.

Roksa, R. A. a. J. (2011), *Academically Adrift: Limited Learning on College Campuses*, Chicago: The University of Chicago Press.

Ross, J. (2021), 'Gag Clauses "Becoming the Norm" in Australian Redundancies', *Times Higher Education*. https://www.timeshighereducation.com/news/gag-clauses-becoming-norm-australian-redundancies#:~:text=Times%20Higher%20Education%20has%20obtained,the%20discussions%20leading%20to%20them..

Rowe, M. B. (1974), 'Pausing Phenomena: Influence on the Quality of Instruction', *Journal of Psycholinguistic Research*, 3 (3): 203–24.

Schwartz, R. (2021), *No Bad Parts: Healing Trauma and Restoring Wholeness with the Internal Family Systems Model*, Boulder: Sounds True.

Scott, J. C. (1990), *Domination and the Arts of Resistance: Hidden Transcripts*, New Haven: Yale University Press.

Sheffer, S. (1995), *A Sense of Self - Listening to Home Schooled Adolescent Girls*, Portsmouth, New Hampshire: Boynton/Cook Publishers.

Smyth, J., ed. (1995), *Academic Work: The Changing Labour Process in Higher Education*, London: Society for Research into Higher Education.

Smyth, J. (2018), *The Toxic University: Zombie Leadership, Academic Rock Stars and Neoliberal Ideology*, London: MacMillan.

Steimer, T. (2002), 'The Biology of Fear- and Anxiety-Related Behaviors', *Dialogues in Clinical Neuroscience*, 4 (3): 231–49.

Stein, S. (2020), 'On the Possibility of Higher Education Otherwise', *Medium.com*. Available online: https://medium.com/@educationotherwise/on-the-possibility-of-higher-education-otherwise-19fe45ffb370.

Stevens, M. L. (2007), *Creating a Class: College Admissions and the Education of Elites*, Cambridge, MA: Harvard University Press.

Suits, B. (1978), *The Grasshopper: Games, Life and Utopia*, Toronto: University of Toronto Press.

Thomas, A. and H. Pattison (2007), *How Children Learn at Home*, London: Continuum.

Thomas, A. and H. Pattison (2013), 'Informal Home Education: Philosophical Aspirations put into Practice', *Studies in Philosophy and Education*, 32 (2): 141–54.

Thorley, C. (2017), *Not by Degrees: Improving Student Mental Health in the UK's Universities*. London: Institute for Public Policy Research. https://www.ippr. org/publications/not-by-degrees.

Tsabar, B. (2014), 'Resistance and Imperfection as Educational Work: Going Against the "Harmony" of Individualistic Ideology', *Other Education*, 3 (1): 23–40.

Tsabar, B. (2021), 'In Favor of Ambiguity: Towards an Existentially Sensitive Pedagogy', *Other Education*, 10 (1): 4–19.

Watts, M. and D. Bridges (2006), 'The Value of Non-Participation in Higher Education', *Journal of Education Policy*, 21 (3): 267–90.

Wilkins, A. and P. J. Burke (2015), 'Widening Participation in Higher Education: The Role of Professional and Social Class Identities and Commitments', *British Journal of Sociology of Education*, 36 (3): 434–52.

Wilkinson, R. and K. Pickett (2009), *The Spirit Level: Why More Equal Societies Almost Always Do Better*, London: Allen Lane.

Willis, P. E. (1981), *Learning to Labour: How Working Class Kids Get Working Class Jobs*, New York: Columbia University Press.

Wittgenstein, L. (1992), *Philosophical Investigations*, Oxford: Blackwell.

Yoneyama, S. (1999), *The Japanese High School: Silence and Resistance*, London: Routledge.

Yoneyama, S. (2000), 'Student Discourse on Tokokyohi (School Phobia/Refusal) in Japan: burnout or empowerment?', *British Journal of Sociology of Education*, 21 (1): 77–94.

Yoneyama, S. and A. Naito (2003), 'Problems with the Paradigm: The School as a Factor in Understanding Bullying (With Special Reference to Japan)', *British Journal of Sociology of Education*, 24 (3): 315–30.

Yorke, J. (2014), *Into The Woods: How Stories Work and Why We Tell Them*, London: Penguin.

Zembylas, M. and P. Michaelides (2004), 'The Sound of Silence in Pedagogy', *Educational Theory*, 54 (2): 193–210.

Index